MW00572155

HOUSE
LOVE

HOUSE
LOVE

A Joyful Guide to Cleaning, Organizing, and Loving the Home You're In

PATRIC RICHARDSON
WITH KARIN B. MILLER

HARVEST
An Imprint of WILLIAM MORROW

HarperCollins books may be purchased for educational, business, or sales promotional use. For information, please email the Special Markets Department at SPsales@harpercollins.com.

FIRST EDITION

Designed by Tai Blanche

Illustrations by Zachary Harris

Library of Congress Cataloging-in-Publication Data has been applied for.

ISBN 978-0-06-327842-4

23 24 25 26 27 LBC 5 4 3 2 1

To my dad, who taught me the
bones of a house. To my mom, who
taught me the beauty of a house.
And to Ross, who taught me home.

AUTHORS' NOTE

Every tip in *House Love* is tried and true. However, you know your home, so please proceed with a careful hand. Patric Richardson and Karin B. Miller are not responsible for any damages arising from following directions inaccurately (due perhaps to not wearing your glasses while reading the aforementioned book), cleaning your home while under the influence (though a little vodka can come in handy when wiping down granite countertops), housecleaning acts of God, etc. The reader assumes sole responsibility for cleaning processes. Cleaning your house isn't rocket science, but it is domestic science. Thank you so much for your attention.

CONTENTS

INTRODUCTION

Ah! There is nothing like staying at home for real comfort.

—Jane Austen, *Emma*

I'm known both as the Laundry Evangelist and the Laundry Guy, but my love of home reaches far beyond the laundry room. I've been enthralled by homes since childhood—and especially since my parents allowed the teenage me to choose my bedroom décor—toasty brown painted walls, a mallard duck wallpaper border (it was the '80s, after all), and hunter-green carpet.

Having been empowered to make those decisions, I'd go on to personalize every home I'd live in, including my first cozy (read: tiny) apartment in a former 1920s mansion in Lexington, Kentucky, and my current historic brownstone in St. Paul, Minnesota. Each presented new opportunities to create home.

Especially fun in my twenties and thirties—even today, honestly—was rising above any budget challenges by breaking rules: Using coat hooks as a tie rack, a lion door knocker as a towel ring, and a kitchen table as a nightstand. Making curtains out of a remnant of twill from a discount store. Screwing stylish gold finials into a cheap metal pipe spray-painted black. Keeping my kitchen utensils in a flowerpot. I swear: Armed with a curtain rod, brown kraft paper, and grosgrain ribbon, I could conquer the world.

Plus, I love—truly love!—cleaning my home. My cleaning credo is similar to the gospel I share regarding laundry: Doing laundry is a privilege and a task you do for those you love, including yourself. Similarly, I aim to always be grateful for a place to lay my head. Not everyone is so lucky. And so it's a blessing and a privilege to be able to have a home to clean and to keep in good repair. Plus, I'm physically able to clean my home. That's also not true for everyone.

For many years now, I've stocked Mona Williams, my store at Mall of America, with vintage fashion and all the laundry items needed to take good care of textiles, but also with home décor, holiday ornaments, and much more, including all-purpose natural cleaners, handcrafted brooms and brushes, and other traditional and modern home-cleaning tools.

When Laundry Campers attend my popular two-hour classes— complete with domestic science, demos, know-how, philosophy, and a humorous story or three—they often spot these items and ask for more information. Many attendees are surprised to head home with not only laundry advice and gear but also great products and ideas for renewing their homes quickly and easily in a morning or an afternoon. And their interest in these items has grown recently.

These days we're spending more time than ever in our homes—for many of us, our personal lives and our work lives now overlap. It's like a throwback to medieval times when serfs lived and worked in their thatched-roof homes—their rooms serving myriad functions. A bedroom, for example, was for sleeping, working, reading, socializing, and more. These days, the same can be said of nearly any space in our homes. The kitchen becomes homework central. The den morphs into the laundry room as you fold clothes while watching *The Golden Girls*. (Did you know the average sofa can hold the clothes from nine laundry baskets?) And the laundry room does double duty as a yoga studio. We're looking at our homes with fresh eyes and seeking new ways to revamp our spaces.

In the pages that follow, we'll delve into every space in your house as I offer novel hacks to clean your home, save money, and be good to the environment; countless ways to freshen up your spaces and elevate your everyday living; and stories to inspire you and perhaps make you laugh.

Each chapter begins with a story or two to inspire your own home design, followed by lots of ideas to refresh your living spaces, and then easy, inexpensive, and often fun how-to instructions for deep cleaning. I conclude each chapter with a get-the-job-done ten-minute clean—complete with a music playlist to clean by.

Throughout the book, you'll find lots of how-to sidebars (like a dozen ways to refresh your living room and three tools to splurge on to make cleaning more effective) plus practical and sometimes surprising tips to make your life easier. And couldn't we all use that?!

As a kid, I was introduced to home-keeping and home décor. As an adult, I'm thankful for my wonderful home and the opportunity to create a space I love to live in. With this book, I'm honored to share my love of home with you.

MY CAST OF CHARACTERS

Complicated novels often employ a cheat sheet of characters, reminding you who everyone is, particularly those secondary folks who only pop up once every fifty pages or so. I took the same approach with my first book, *Laundry Love: Finding Joy in a Common Chore*, and I'm offering up bios here as well. ("Who's Louise again?") So, taking my cue from Tolstoy, my list includes personal descriptions, each one's relationship to myself, and the celebrity or character who comes to mind when I think of each. After all, if my life were a house, I'd fill it with all the people I love. Feel free to refer back to the list whenever needed.

Mom: Her friends know her as Wilma, but she's always Mom to me. She and my dad gave me an incredible childhood and influenced me in many ways, perhaps most especially with their desire to make everyone feel welcome in our home. Mom is the ultimate hostess and the queen of graciousness, putting everyone at ease when they visit. Not long ago, we went on vacation together and, sure enough, she played hostess when I visited her hotel room, offering me a slice of pound cake that she'd baked and brought along. As I've said before, she's like Jackie Kennedy—in leopard print and with a Southern drawl. And like Jackie, she would've whipped that White House into shape in no time. Her philosophy: A neat, clean, well-appointed home is a happy one.

Dad: I owe my understanding of how houses work to Dad, aka Ron. He was working as a boilermaker when he decided on a new career: building houses. The first home he ever built was my childhood house, and he was off to the races—an apt metaphor, considering we lived in Kentucky, home of the Derby. As a kid, I loved looking at his blueprints and visiting his construction sites. He was forward thinking too, introducing new approaches to his houses long before they were regular practices—tasks like placing phone jacks, and later cable jacks, in every room; adding utility sinks in mudrooms and garages; and creating multiple heat zones by using more than one heat pump. I also learned from Dad to pay a little more up front for good-quality home items. He'd say, "You'll forget what you paid, but you'll enjoy it forever." (Plus, you'll rarely have to replace those items, so you'll actually save money in the long run.) For example, my first "big boy" bed is now in my mom's guest room. Dad's philosophy: Set up your house to live in it. Really live in it. As for the characters who remind me of my dad, I'd say Jonathan Hart from *Hart to Hart* or a really nice J. R. Ewing from *Dallas*, both popular 1980s TV shows.

Jarrod: My little brother started working for my dad as a kid, soaking up his knowledge like a sponge. And while Jarrod's a social worker, in his personal life he's the go-to guy if you're building anything. He's built more decks, additions, and garages for his friends than I can count. And like our granddad, he's a tinkerer. He's the first person I call when I need to fix something and don't know how. Jarrod either knows how to do that something or knows someone who knows how to do that something. He's Mr. Fix-It to a T. And like our parents, Jarrod is kind and giving, always jumping in to help others.

Granny Dude: While her given name was Irene, I always called my mom's mom Granny Dude. When I was four, my family moved in with her while we were building our house next door. And I quickly saw that everyone loved to stop by to visit her—she considered everyone family. I completely adored her, and I know she felt the same about me. Throughout my school years, I'd stop by her house to see her on my way home every day. As an adult, I moved home for a year when my mom and Granny Dude were living together—I'm so lucky to have had that time with her. If she were still with us, I know she would've loved the ten-minute clean options in the pages ahead! And once again, I look to *Dallas* for a character—Granny Dude was like Miss Ellie.

Granny Martha: Old-fashioned and Appalachian, Granny Martha and Grandpa, my dad's parents, lived about a half hour from our house, and I used to stay with them many weekends. Their house was midcentury modern with an open concept and no formal parlor. There was no pretense in that house—comfort was key. In my mind's eye, I always think of her in a day dress and an apron, cooking down-home, delicious meals for my grandpa's workers and keeping the coffee percolating all day. She'd have fit in perfectly as Grandma Walton on *The Waltons*. Oh, and she made the fluffiest, most amazing corn bread stuffing ever—no one can replicate her recipe, try as we have.

Nancy: Nancy is married to my dad, but calling her a stepmother sounds cold and impersonal. From the time I met her when I was twelve, she has been warm and loving. While she worked as a banker, she's a true homemaker—her home is always neat, her food is always amazing, and she loves to make everyone around her happy, starting with my dad. (We're all lucky he met her.) If you visit, she'll have your favorite food waiting. Mine is her Chex mix. Her grandkids love Ale-8, a Kentucky ginger-citrus soft drink. While they live out of state, she always has cases on hand for whenever they visit. Think of her as Mrs. Brady, aka Florence Henderson on *The Brady Bunch*.

Ruby: Ruby lived on the hill where I grew up. I always loved her travel stories and big-city ways. She taught me many lessons about style and polish that I still use today. What she understood so well was the importance of creating spaces you can enjoy, personalizing your décor, and making cleaning easy. For example, she purchased three vacuums, one for each level of her house. That sounds like an indulgent choice, but she knew she was much more likely to sweep if the vacuum cleaners were easily accessible. She displayed her knick-knacks in a glass-fronted case, so she rarely had to dust them. And she kept a basket of towels on her patio, so she could wipe down her outdoor furniture right after a rain. I learned so much from her about making daily life great, and every time I watch the film *Mame*, I think of her.

Louise: My mom's middle name is Louise because of Louise—a friend of Granny Dude and Granddad's. Always single, Louise treated my mother like a really lucky niece, and I grew up thinking of her as a bonus grandmother. She lived in the same house nearly her entire life, updating it to suit her needs as she grew older; she lived on her own until she passed at ninety-three. Louise could also do anything with fabric, yarn, and thread: She made clothes, knit-ted, crocheted, embroidered, did needlepoint, and more. One reason I love doing needlepoint today is because of her. Think of her as that older, fun, and wise neighbor in every Hallmark movie you've ever seen.

Ross: My love is the funny one, the one who allows me to follow my passions, the one who makes me want to clean, do laundry, and breathe. Ross is the reason I want to make my house a home. And despite the chaos of home projects, he always appreciates the results. When I met Ross in 2005, he told me that I should write a book. Now I've got two. These books, like my story, aren't complete without Ross in them. In fact, for this book, Ross, a longtime pop music critic, was an integral creator of the song lists you'll find throughout the book. I couldn't have made them without his musical insights and creativity. Think of, well, I think of perfection when I think of him, so think of whomever that is to you.

TOOL UP

Novelist's Wife: Why does your heroine "enter and sweep the room with a glance"?

Novelist (scornfully): Because she has no vacuum cleaner.

—Town Topics, *Daily Times*, Barre, Vermont, December 26, 1907

Having the right tools and knowing how to use them makes home cleaning easier, faster, and, most important, fun. It also helps if your tools are attractive and of high quality—in fact, I've found that good-looking, well-made tools often inspire more frequent cleaning sessions (more on that later). In the meantime, let's detail all the supplies I use daily, plus the household appliances I've splurged on to make my life easier. I also list nice-to-have cleaning tools that can make any chore a snap.

Start by gathering "The Essentials" listed next—you probably own most, if not all, of them already. By having these on hand, you won't have to buy and use a bunch of (potentially harmful) chemicals, and your cleaning will be just as thorough. As for the items on the other two lists, I don't recommend going out and buying everything. Rather, just get the items you'll use regularly. Most of the time, you can make do with what you've got. And honestly, you can clean any home top to bottom with "The Essentials"—you might have to use a bit more sweat equity, but you can get the job done.

The Essentials

- 50/50 distilled white vinegar–water solution in a spray bottle
- Baking soda
- Dish soap
- Vodka (the cheap stuff)
- Old kitchen towels or a bag of rags from a hardware store
- Broom and dustpan
- Treat to eat while you're cleaning (I prefer MoonPies)

VINEGAR 101

Just like Granny Dude and Granny Martha, and likely your grandmas too, I clean practically everything with a powerful solution of 50 percent vinegar and 50 percent water. In fact, all those grandmothers wielding *vin aigre* (that's French for sour wine) stretch back two hundred generations. It's true: People have been tapping vinegar for cleaning, cooking, preserving, and much more for five thousand years.

So what's this miracle concoction? Vinegar is roughly 90 percent water and 10 percent acetic acid, the latter of which is created through fermentation, thanks to tiny micro-organisms processing naturally occurring ethanol. You can think of this simple solution as a superhero, swooping in with a spray bottle and a cape (or a rag) to eliminate dirt, fingerprints, grease, mineral deposits, and much more. Its acidic oomph even kills bacteria.

What does the 50/50 white vinegar–water solution lack? The high price tags of commercial cleaners and their nearly unpronounceable chemical ingredients—chemicals that are often harmful to you, your loved ones, your home, and the environment. Plus, when you buy one giant jug of vinegar, which lasts for months, and a few spray bottles that last for years, you avoid consuming those numerous plastic containers that commercial cleaners are packaged in.

You can also make your own scented vinegar: Add orange, lemon, or grapefruit peels to a glass quart jar. Pour in the vinegar, replace the lid, and shake the jar for thirty seconds or so. Now let that jar sit in a warm or room-temperature space (not in an unheated garage, for example) for three weeks. Then strain out the peels, and you've got citrus-scented vinegar—at a fraction of the price of store-bought scented vinegar! Bonus: It now includes citric acid, which makes it an even stronger cleaner. Or you can add thyme to vinegar, which delivers thymol and antibacterial properties. Other organic add-ins include cinnamon sticks, peppermint leaves, pine needles, sprigs of rosemary, and vanilla beans. Also, if you like a stronger scent, you can always add a few drops of your favorite essential oil to scented or plain old vinegar.

P.S.: What shouldn't you clean with vinegar? Granite and stone.

Three Splurges

Cordless tool system: Not long ago, my tools—orbital buffer, drill, shop vacuum, Weedwacker, and more—were made by a bunch of manufacturers. Buying all the different batteries wasted time and effort. So I converted to one brand. Now, whenever I buy a new tool, I stick to that brand. That means my batteries are interchangeable, and I've always got a couple charged and ready to go.

To choose your tool brand, compare the tools you need with those offered by various manufacturers. I don't necessarily recommend buying a tool kit, as it's likely to include items you'll never use. Just buy the tools you need.

Steam cleaner: If you've never used a steamer—prepare yourself: Steamers are miracle workers and addictive in the best way. In your kitchen, for example, drips of jam are gone in a jiffy, Diet Coke spills disappear, and grout simply glows. How does it work? Steam disinfects, sanitizes, degreases, deodorizes, and, best of all, cleans with heat instead of chemicals.

You can either buy a $50 budget steamer that'll get the job done, or spring for a $150 canister steamer that holds more water for cleaning sessions that can last up to an hour. If you do decide to invest in a tool that you think you'll use, I recommend spending a little more to get a tool that makes cleaning extra easy. Over time, you'll forget how much you paid, but your cleaning routine will continue to be all the easier.

Regardless of which model you buy, your steamer attachments will beg the question: What will you clean first? Will you squeegee your mirrors, shower walls, and windows? (I even clean the exterior windows that I can reach.) Will you mop your floors—tile, vinyl, even sealed hardwood? Perhaps you'll grab the small pads to clean your grout or the bigger pads to bring your upholstered furniture back to life. Maybe you'll fasten on the triangle pads to get into corners that haven't been cleaned in forever, or spray clean your tub and toilets? (You can even steam your car seats.) Then, when your rooms are gleaming, just throw the mop and any pads—zipped up in mesh bags, of course—right into the washing machine and allow them to air-dry so they're ready for the next time.

Stick vacuum—cordless and rechargeable: Hardly a day goes by that I don't reach for this genius tool. I'd wanted one forever, and when it fell to half price on a Black Friday, I raced to the store. Worlds easier to use than a corded vacuum, it's lightweight and requires no bags, which saves money. Best of all, vacuuming steps isn't a sweaty workout—or a life-and-death situation, since you don't drag that tripping hazard of a cord behind you. Cordless vacuums feature just as many attachments as corded vacuums. Plus, you can tuck it away in a closet within reach of the spaces that need regular vacuuming. And with all these great attributes, you're apt to use it often. *Vroom, vroom!*

HL Tip: Even in a small home or an apartment, you need hand tools. If you're just getting started, consider this quartet: a hammer, a flathead screwdriver, a Phillips screwdriver, and a pair of pliers. For a deep discount, snap up these tools at estate sales. (Who said thrifting is only for clothes and Christmas ornaments? At least that's what I buy.) One other tool that I recommend and often give as a graduation present is a multi-tool. This compact device, similar to a Swiss Army knife, features cutters, knives, openers, pliers, saws, and screwdrivers, all of which fold into the handle.

xxiv • TOOL UP

The Nice-to-Haves

Brooms, specialty: Did you know that different types of brooms have different purposes? When do you need a heavy-duty broom, an angle broom, or a push broom? How about a corn, straw, or handheld broom? Selecting the best brooms for your needs can be nearly as confusing as buying a mattress. So here's the lowdown:

- Got a garage or patio? Then I highly recommend a push broom, known for its wide brush and centered handle. It's great at sweeping up large areas, and it only needs a few passes to get the whole space clean. No garage or patio? Then cross this one off your shopping list.

- If you've got tile and/or luxury vinyl, buy a stiff broom. A standard corn or straw broom works well for this purpose. If you regularly sweep off a front porch, a deck, or a sidewalk, a biodegradable and sustainable coir broom (made from coconut husks) comes in handy. Also, dedicating a broom to outdoor spaces makes sense—you don't want all that dirt contaminating your indoors.

- For all other floors, especially hardwood, rely on a horsehair broom. They last forever, their bristles are soft, they won't scratch your floor, and they're phenomenal for picking up dust and dirt. As for cost, the more horsehair that's packed into the head of a broom, the higher the price. But any horsehair broom—standard or angle—performs well, and the latter works well in corners.

- Near my fireplace, I keep a hand broom in a basket with other fireplace tools, like fire starters, matches, etc. If you've got a wood-burning fireplace, this is a handy little tool.

- Oh, and don't forget a dustpan—I recommend using a contractor's metal version from a hardware store. It's heavy enough that you don't have to hold it while sweeping, and, because it's wider than a standard broom, you only need a single sweep to push your entire dust pile into it. Plus, it should cost less than twenty bucks. Now that's a good deal for a long-lasting tool.

- The only broom I don't fully understand is the Nimbus 2000. That's a wizard-style broom you're unlikely to need—although wouldn't it be cool to fly one?

Brushes: Load up on a bunch of brushes to make cleaning easy: two small horsehair brushes for polishing such things as silverware and picture frames, and three or four Tampico and/or coir brushes for cleaning the kitchen and bathroom: e.g., a long-handled dish brush, a short-handled pot brush, and a long-handled toilet brush. Tampico is a biodegradable, acid-resistant fiber made from Mexican agave plants; coir is an antimicrobial, decay-resistant fiber made from coconuts; both are better for the environment than a plastic brush. I'd also recommend hanging on to an old toothbrush (preferably an environmentally friendly, compostable bamboo toothbrush) for scrubbing around faucets.

Buckets: Some ice creams come packed in gallon tubs. But don't confuse an ice cream tub with a bucket that can assist with lots of household jobs. Instead, buy a couple of good-quality buckets. They come in a gazillion sizes. I recommend buying the largest one your storage space—say, under the laundry sink—can accommodate. Galvanized buckets are made of steel coated with zinc to prevent rust. These are heavy enough not to tip over—whether filled with soapy water for washing the car or loaded with ice and a variety of beverages for a party. A plastic bucket, meanwhile, can pull double duty as a tool caddy—great for carrying cleaning supplies throughout the house. Of course, you can purchase a tool caddy, but why not just use a bucket and save money? At some point you're going to need a bucket, and then you'll have one. And if you're going to buy a plastic bucket, why not buy it in a fun color? I suggest orange, my favorite.

Buffer, orbital: You may be asking: What the heck is an orbital buffer? Answer: Possibly the best tool you've never heard of. This handheld powered machine is used to polish and clean hard surfaces. You can find corded and cordless (my preference) versions. While often used to buff cars, it's also a phenomenal household tool, packing a lot of power despite its relatively small size—they can weigh anywhere from two to eight pounds depending on the model.

For the cleanest bathtub ever, use a buffer to clean your tub once a season. Buh-bye, soap scum. Use the buffer to wax your wood floors a couple of times a year for incredible results—there's no need to refinish your floors. Or buff up your grimy handrails or dingy wood

HL Tip: Some apartment-management companies offer a tool library, and why not? It's likely that tenants will keep their living spaces cleaner if tools are accessible. But if your dorm, apartment building, or other communal living situation doesn't provide a tool library, consider starting one yourself. The idea? Each person buys one tool—vacuum, rug shampooer, etc.—and shares, saving you all money and storage space. Impressively, in the Twin Cities, where I live, there's also the Minnesota Tool Library, which boasts five thousand items, including such cleaning tools as a pressure washer, a garment steamer, and a leaf blower, plus brooms, dustpans, and more.

furniture. Got granite countertops? Use the orbital buffer to seal them in a flash. I've even used my buffer on a leather letter jacket. Where can't you use a buffer? Soon, that's the question you'll be asking. This little genius can be had for as little as forty bucks, or invest in a bit more expensive model that's part of a cordless tool system.

Cleaners: Ninety-nine percent of the time I rely on dish soap, vinegar, and vodka for all my cleaning. But in a pinch, I turn to another trio: Amodex, check. Bar Keepers Friend, check. Silver polish, check. Amodex, an all-natural formulation made by a family-owned company for more than sixty years, removes permanent inks and dyes—super handy if you get a bit of Sharpie on your favorite shirt. Use Bar Keepers Friend when you want to clean that porcelain sink until it's pristine. And silver polish is good for, well, you know. If you don't own sterling, you don't need it.

Cloths: While a bag of rags and old kitchen towels are great for cleaning, don't throw out old terrycloth bathroom towels. They're also super for cleaning, especially in the bathroom. Plus, if you make a few cuts along the side of a bathroom towel with a sharp pair of scissors, rip away and you've got several nice-sized rags. Having a few microfiber cloths are helpful as well, especially if you're allergic to dust.

Dusters: Oh, how I love a colorful yarn mop—both for its aesthetics and its magnetic ability to grab dust and pet hair! That's thanks to the lanolin in the wool yarn. Handheld wool dusters and feather dusters are equally great for dusting furniture. To clean the wool items, simply drop them into a mesh bag, secure with rubber bands or safety pins so the wool items don't move around in the wash, and launder. To clean the feather duster, just whack it against an outdoor wall or on a deck rail.

CREATE A CLEANING CLOSET

I'm by no means a neat freak. But when it comes to organizing my tools and cleaners, I find it super helpful to place them all together in one closet. Having one centralized location means that whenever I need to quickly mop up a spill or reach for my cordless stick vacuum, I'm not looking all over the house and can find everything together. I even store my drill in the cleaning closet because I use the brush attachment to clean my bathtub more often than I use the drill for woodworking projects.

It's here too where I keep my giant jugs of vinegar, my spray bottles, my microfiber cloths, and my old dish towels. And in addition to my stick vacuum, I store here a handheld Dustbuster, a broom, a dustpan, and a lambswool duster. It's kind of like a pantry for tools and you can treat it as such, replenishing supplies as they run out and adding battery-operated puck lights to make finding items extra easy.

Plungers: I'm going to let you in on a secret: There are two types of plungers—if you didn't know that before, you're now in the know. The half-a-bagel plunger (some look like accordions) is designed to unclog slow-moving drains in sinks, tubs, and showers. The heavy-duty ball style, meanwhile, provides major plunging power to clear tough toilet clogs. In a pinch, either can be used for the other purpose. But it's better, and more sanitary, to use each for the task for which it was designed.

LOOKING AND FEELING GOOD WHILE DOING THE DIRTY WORK

Now's the perfect time to wear that Culture Club T-shirt you picked up at the state fair. That's my cleaning tee of choice. It makes me happy to pull it on—and that's how I suggest you choose your cleaning attire. Just like any activity, I find dressing the part sets the mood—like wearing fitness clothes to work out, overalls to garden, or a tuxedo to shop at the grocery store (or maybe that's just me?). When you're about to embark on a chore sesh, your clothes should make you smile. As for the rest of your cleaning attire and gear, here are my suggestions:

- **One great ball cap.** When you need to clean something up close, say a dusty corner under a lower kitchen cabinet, just flip that brim backward.
- **One pair of colorful socks.** Keeping a sense of humor while cleaning can be helpful, especially if you share a home with particularly messy companions. Plus, socks do double-duty as dusters when you slide around your floors.
- **One large insulated tumbler.** Staying hydrated is always a good idea. I prefer to fill mine with Diet Coke, and I wasn't paid to say so.
- **One pair of earbuds.** Stream great tunes to groove to as you clean. Doing chores burns up to three hundred calories an hour, so imagine if you're dancing how many more calories you'll scorch as you scrub. Or skip the earbuds and blast those tunes on a speaker so the whole household can twirl as they clean.

Sponges: For sanitary purposes, keep two sponges on hand—one for the kitchen and one for the rest of the house. Throw them in the dishwasher to clean and replace every four months or so. I recommend earth-friendly options, like those made from recycled cotton, former coffee sacks, or vegetable cellulose—often coconuts, loofah gourds, or walnuts. These sponges are generally biodegradable and compostable, and they don't contain toxic chemicals that take decades to break down.

Vacuum, hand: I've got two hand vacuums—one for upstairs and one for downstairs. And, no, I'm not lazy (at least not most of the time). I just want each one ready at a moment's notice.

Vacuum, robot: If your spaces are like mine with a random sock or newspaper on the floor, maybe this one's not for you. However, if your spaces are nice and neat, this machine might be the perfect choice. Just turn it on and let it go. (If it comes back to you, it was meant to be.)

CHAPTER 1

ENTRYWAY
YOU'RE MORE THAN WELCOME

*Welcome to my house! Enter freely. Go safely, and leave
something of the happiness you bring!*

—Bram Stoker, *Dracula*

Everybody's heard about the importance of making a great first impression. It's a cliché but true. The same thing can be said about your home. And it's your entryway that offers a first handshake to visitors. Hello—great to meet you. The foyer also greets you, the person who lives there. Nice to see you again—welcome home! At least that's how we all should feel every time we step inside our homes.

I begin this chapter with the most spectacular entryway I ever set foot in—at least as a kid. I share four things that make every entry more inviting, I offer ideas for freshening up your space, and I detail how to make it shine in less than ten minutes. Let's get started.

Getting Inspired

Long ago, my mom, our friend Susie, my cousin Bethany, and my six-year-old self were going to optometrist appointments in Ashland, Kentucky—a half-hour drive from our homes in Grayson. I'd never been to the optometrist before, and it turned out the eye doctor's office was not in some strip mall or bland high-rise but in a glamorous Italianate mansion. (If only every doctor and dentist office were located at an expansive estate, perhaps fewer of us would dread our appointments!)

Because I was just a little kid, every detail of this showplace seemed enormous and all the more grand. Remodeled in 1917 by Alice Jane Mayo, who seemingly had all the money in the world to pour into this incredible estate, the Mayo Mansion has been a landmark in Ashland for more than a hundred years. I remember stepping onto the red-and-white checkerboard marble floor and noticing the word *salve* embedded there; later I'd learn that it's the Latin word for *hello*. What a cheerful welcome!

A grand spiral staircase rose up from the floor to the first landing and then to a second landing where the most incredible ceiling made up of colored glass glimmered overhead—it was actually a dome crafted by the famed Tiffany Studios. Oh, and there was also a small glass elevator to the left, plus marble pillars—one after another—flanking the hallway, elaborate woodwork marching its way across the walls, super-tall wooden doors, and, in the waiting area, a lavish brass chandelier. I was mesmerized.

Even at my young age, I'd seen beautiful houses before. My dad was a contractor, and Mom and I would sometimes visit the homes he was building—some quite impressive. But this was different. This was a Beaux Arts mansion—which just means a mishmash of architecture from the French Neoclassicism, Renaissance, and Baroque periods. At my tender age, I just knew it was beautiful.

I never returned as a patient (I didn't need glasses until recently—funny how that happens in, ahem, early middle age), but growing up, I brought up that grand house to my mom every time we'd drive by. Remember that staircase? Remember that elevator? Remember that beautiful ceiling?! That doctor's appointment ranked right up there with Ohio's Kings Island, the best theme park I ever visited as a kid.

HL Tip: My entryway serves a secret purpose: Using the space underneath the table and behind the floor-length tablecloth, I've hidden a shredder. (Don't do this if you've got kids at home or young visitors.) The moment mail comes into our home, we shred the junk mail and envelopes. Some cities' recycling services can process shredded paper, but not all can. If yours can't, consider adding it to your compost pile (no glossy paper or envelope windows), repurposing it as pet bedding and donating it to your local vet, adding it as mulch to planting containers, making homemade paper with it, or using it as packing when shipping presents. (Apropos of nothing, my birthday is November 15.)

Then, as a high school senior, I returned to the Mayo Mansion on a class field trip. By then the mansion was serving as the Highlands Museum, a treasury of cultural and historical exhibits. My fellow students and I were there to study the house itself—all seventeen thousand square feet of it. Climbing that spiral staircase, I quickly found new favorite details: a coved ceiling with curved edges where it met the walls, a third-floor ballroom that featured a fireplace, a Tiffany skylight that ran the length of an upstairs hallway, and another Tiffany installation, this time a waterfall scene in a powder room.

Why share all this with you? Because only recently—in fact, only since researching homes and interiors in preparation for writing this book—did it dawn on me that I've got my own micro Mayo Mansion entryway.

I live in a narrow 1883 brownstone that was actually built prior to the Mayo Mansion. Step inside and you find a black-and-white checkerboard floor. (Nope, it's not marble, but still.) There's a small chandelier sparkling overhead. And while there's no spiral staircase, an impressive set of stairs leads to the second floor—and another to the third floor. And, just like at the Mayo Mansion, double doors lead into the living room. There's no ballroom and no Tiffany glass, but I have no doubt that my love of that dazzling entryway subconsciously influenced my decision to buy this house.

Making an Entrance

Earlier, I mentioned setting the stage. And that's exactly what an entryway does, for better or for worse. That's true whether it's a front door, usually the site of package drop-offs and dinner guests, or the back door, where family and friends pile inside or we head out for our day.

An entryway is anticipatory. It gives visitors a glimpse of what to expect in the rest of your home. That's what's fun about visiting a friend's home for the first time. You step inside and think, "Wow" or "Cool" or "Now that's a surprise. I never would've imagined seeing that inside the front door!"

I also associate anticipation with entryways because of Christmas. I remember as a kid standing (or more likely jumping up and down) with my brother, Jarrod, at the top of the stairs while gazing down at the front door. Our parents didn't allow us to come down the stairs until after Granny Dude and Granddad had carried in all of their Christmas presents and placed them under the tree. In truth, I don't think we were permitted to join them because our grandparents were in cahoots with Santa, quickly tucking away a few gifts for Christmas morning. (One of the most memorable? An Atari game for the two of us a whole year before Atari really hit it big. Granny Dude always loved techy gifts and being ahead of the trends.)

Take a look at your entryway. Does it make you smile? Does it give a hint about the rest of your home? Is it a formal or lively or calming space that welcomes you inside? Or is its beauty hiding under a bunch of coats, a pile of yesterday's mail, and a scattering of shoes and boots? Well, that's to be expected. We lead busy lives. Fortunately, entryways tend to be small and can be whipped into shape quickly.

At my house, there's both a vestibule that you step into from our front door and then the foyer itself. While the rest of my house is all neutrals—blacks, grays, silvers, and tans—the vestibule's ceiling and walls are a vivid, cheerful orange. An oval mahogany mirror with carved laurel leaves invites you to check your appearance as you arrive (or as you leave), and there's one small abstract print. That's it. Because the space is tiny, it's also tidy. And the warmth of the orange feels like a hug as you step inside. (If I ever have the chance to retile, I'm going to work in that Latin word *salve*—oh, and a heated floor.)

Time to Freshen Up

Imagine your entryway right now. What are its colors? What art is included? What items help you start and end your day? What does it feel like when you're standing in the space? I promise: Every entryway can be made more inviting, more welcoming, and more livable by incorporating these four things:

1. something beautiful
2. something scented
3. a place to drop your keys and mail
4. a place to hang up your coat

I bet your entryway has at least a few of these items already. Ensure your foyer features all four items, so you can achieve a beautiful and organized space.

Something beautiful might be an original painting, a framed poster, or your kid's latest creation. Or it might be a colorful wallpaper backdrop, an antique trunk, or a living greenery wall. And there may be overlap; for example, something beautiful might also be something scented, say a glorious bouquet. Or something scented might be a candle or an essential oil diffuser. A place to drop your mail might be a terrific teak tray or a colorful basket, while your keys are plunked on a whimsical hook or dropped into a pottery bowl made by a local artist or a grandchild. And finally, a place to hang up coats might be a small entryway closet, a good-looking hall rack, or a minimalist wooden peg.

While I'm imagining a small-scale entryway—what most of us have in our homes—entryways can make us feel at home, at ease, and welcome even on a grand scale. Not long ago I was staying at the iconic Essex House in New York City. As I walked into the Art Deco lobby, I heard someone yell, "I love you!" And the woman just ahead of me blew kisses in the general direction of the caller.

Despite the glamour of the space, that warm and welcoming environment put me right at ease and, before I knew it, I was joking aloud with both of them: "Now that's how I expect to be greeted!"

The woman ahead of me then turned around to face me. "Yeah, isn't that something?!" she said, smiling. In a flash, I recognized her as a statuesque reality TV star.

"Oh, it's you!" I said with a smile. "I fully understand. But I still expect to be greeted that way." She laughed and we kept chatting until we stepped onto our separate elevators, hers headed to a much higher floor.

Why did this lobby make me feel so welcome and at home—relaxed enough to address strangers? I think, in part, it's because it included all of those four items: standout art and a mirrored table (both beautiful items) topped by a heavenly bouquet (something scented), crystal chandeliers (more beautiful stuff), and a desk clerk to hand you your room key (the designated place for your keys). It even has checkered flooring à la the Mayo Mansion. The only thing missing was a place to hang my coat, but I bet the concierge would've hung on to it for me if I'd asked nicely. Sure, I'm an extrovert, but had that space been cold, sterile, and bland—say, like many a hospital corridor—would I have felt bold enough to address those two strangers? And would that fan have felt courageous enough to yell, "I love you!" in the first place? I doubt it.

The lesson? Whether you've got a twelve-square-foot vestibule or a five-thousand-square-foot lobby, you can achieve a welcoming environment with a few simple details. Take a fresh look at your entryway and consider:

- Does my entryway lack any of the four elements?
- Of the elements I have, do I love all of them?
- What might I add? What might I remove?
- How might any changes make my space more livable?
- Does the entry set the tone for the rest of my home?

Dressing to Impress

Once you understand the various items needed, it's just a matter of finding pieces that work together to complement the rest of your home. Imagine your living room wallpaper as a brightly colored sweater. Just like you use one of the sweater's colors to help you decide on a shirt to wear underneath and another color to select a pair of pants, you can pull a color or two from that living room wallpaper into your foyer. In the same way, you might give a nod to that touch of whimsy in your kitchen in the foyer. Or maybe you like a preppy look? How about your green thumb? You get the idea. The space should be about you and the rest of your home.

Let's consider a couple of entryways as examples: Say you love a funky look, so you hang a velvet Elvis print over a red leather trunk you found at an estate sale. Now you've got two beautiful items. (Yes, he's beautiful. It's the young Elvis after all—a hunk, a hunk of burnin' love.) Next, you top the trunk with a vintage ashtray for your keys and a woven basket for your mail. Fortunately, you've got an entryway closet, so your coats are taken care of. Now you just need something that smells good: maybe a bouquet from the grocery store today and flowers from your garden next week.

Or maybe your foyer offers a twist on a traditional look, with striped wallpaper and a horse-themed print, both in an updated color palette, like Warhol pop colors. But your entryway is so tiny that you can barely change your mind let alone your shoes in the space. No worries. A gilded mirror (something beautiful) instantly makes the space look larger—plus, it lets you take a quick peek at yourself as you head out the door. (Coco Chanel is widely quoted as saying, "Before you leave the house, look in the mirror and take one thing off." I always suggest adding one more.) A super-narrow Queen Anne console takes up little floor space but accommodates a narrow lacquered tray perfect for your mail, your keys, and a citrus candle (something scented). And a trio of hooks takes care of your coat, hat, and handbag. (My friend Mary would flip if I'd written "purse." Her rule: "You purse your lips. You carry a handbag.")

While your entryway may look lovely and feel inviting, it also does some heavy lifting, accommodating coats, shoes, hats, and more. Most homes—from condos to castles—have an entryway closet. But if storage space in your home is golden, consider using that closet to store off-season jackets, cleaning supplies, even your vacuum. Then dedicate a few wall hooks for the coats and hats you're wearing each season. A friend with three kids keeps a giant basket in her entryway—in the summer, it holds baseball caps; in the winter, it's piled high with hats, mittens, and gloves.

If you've got a bit more space, a hat rack or coatrack can hold all these items, plus those of visitors. Numerous styles and sizes of racks exist, from ones hung on walls to traditional single-pole styles.

Then there are more substantial pieces of furniture called hall trees; they come in all styles and sizes, from freestanding minimalist versions to built-in traditional styles and elaborate antique models. First made popular in the late 1800s before hallway closets were popularized, this one-man-band of the entryway usually features a mirror, hooks, a bench, and cubbies to hold hats, coats, bags, umbrellas, walking sticks, and more.

HL Tip: Here's a fun and stylish idea for your rain and snow boots: Buy a couple of jelly-roll pans, which feature straight edges, and line them up in your entryway. Fill them with smooth river rocks (you can buy a bag of them at a landscape nursery). Then set those wet or snowy boots atop these trays; the water will drip right through to the bottom of the pans rather than drip onto your floor. Periodically, just rinse off the stones and the pans, and return them to the entryway.

Today, prices range the gamut, from a couple of hundred dollars for a new wood hall tree to thousands of dollars for antique versions—often hand-carved out of walnut or mahogany, or cast of iron—possessing drawers, marble shelves, and even hidden compartments. In many newer houses, some version of a hall tree is often employed in the mudroom, whether freestanding or built right in.

Looking back at my early love for the Mayo Mansion entryway, it turns out I'm still smitten. And for good reason: That space opened my eyes to possibilities—not only for what a foyer might look like but also for décor, size, scale, functionality, and more.

What comes to mind for you as your dream entryway? I hope it's your own—or will be soon. Or perhaps it's one that made an impression on you long ago? Maybe a friend's entryway you saw during a childhood playdate, perhaps one in a snug cabin you visited as a teen, a beachy or modern entryway you saw on vacation, or, like me, the foyer of a historic mansion. Close your eyes and imagine it. Go ahead, I'll wait.

Now think about what feeling you want your own entryway to convey. What's waiting for you as you open the door? How does it feel as you walk in? What do you see on the floor, the walls, the ceiling?

This book is all about helping you achieve such visions. Maybe you're not in love with your current home or your current entryway. Remember that Stephen Stills song "Love the One You're With"? You may move to another home or several in your future. But meanwhile, it's time to love the one you're in, to live as if you love this current home. And beginning with your entryway is a great place to start. Thanks to your personal choices, your entryway can be as unique and beautiful as you are.

Time to Clean Up

When's the best time to clean this welcoming space? Right after ordering delivery of egg drop soup and cashew chicken on a Friday night. While the rest of the house is a bit Grey Gardens—Legos scattered all over the living room floor and dishes piled high in the kitchen sink—your newly cleaned entryway will feel peaceful and calm. No doubt your delivery person will think you live like Jackie O., her incredibly stylish sister, Lee, or Beyoncé.

- First, if you keep any shoes or boots in the entryway, set them all aside, along with the rug, the floor mat, and any coats hung on hooks. Moving these items now will prevent dust from landing on them.
- Return any odd items—a coffee mug, a spoon, a book—to their homes, and deliver the mail to wherever it belongs in the house (perhaps the shredder).
- Next, grab your feather duster and dust the light fixture overhead. If any light bulbs are on the blink or burned out, now's a great time to replace them.
- Moving downward, dust your art, the mirror, items on the entryway table, the table itself, your hall tree, or anything else in the space.
- Next, spray a microfiber cloth or old newspaper with a 50/50 vinegar-water solution, and clean the mirror, glass-framed artwork, and any other glass items.
- Now that the floor is dusty (and perhaps dirty as well), vacuum or sweep, scooping up any dust and dirt into a dustpan and throwing it out. Once every couple of months, grab your steam cleaner and give your floor a good cleaning. At my first vintage clothing store in Minneapolis, I began using a steam cleaner—I didn't want a wet mop near my clothes—and it removed salt, shoeprints, and

SHOES OR NO SHOES?

Learning about entryways in other cultures can help inform our choices. Let's consider the traditional Japanese genkan. (While I'm by no means an expert, I admire and respect Japanese culture.) A genkan is an entryway where homeowners and visitors remove their shoes. Traditionally, doing so ensured families didn't track dirt onto the tatami, or straw mats. This tradition is found elsewhere too. When I moved to Minnesota, I'd been invited to a friend's house and was hanging out in the living room when another friend alerted me that I should've removed my shoes in the entryway.

While few Minnesotans keep a tatami room, the northern climate does feature snow, ice, mud, and dirt. So it's no wonder most follow the shoe-removal practice. I even know of a woman who keeps a basketful of loaner slippers in her entryway during the winter months for visitors with cold tootsies.

Asking visitors to remove shoes is practically unheard of among the Southerners I grew up with. Indeed, I can't imagine Granny Dude or my mom asking anyone to remove their shoes. But maybe they should have. According to environmental chemists Mark Patrick Taylor and Gabriel Filippelli ("Wearing Shoes in the House Is Gross," *The Washington Post*, April 3, 2022), who've studied the practice, they say "about a third of [the matter building up inside your home] is from outside, either blown in or tramped in on those offensive shoe bottoms." This includes drug-resistant pathogens, difficult-to-treat germs, cancer-causing asphalt road residue, endocrine-disrupting lawn chemicals, and potentially toxic metals. For that matter, they also recommend wiping off your pets' paws before they come indoors.

I've never been a fan of removing shoes—they make my outfit after all. But now that I know this, I may come around.

---

dirt amazingly well. (Today, I even use it to clean my front door—fingerprints disappear like magic.)

- Before returning a rug and/or mat to the entryway, shake it out-doors or over a trash can. Then return the shoes and boots to the space, lining them up neatly.
- If you've got a bouquet, throw out any dead flowers or leaves, trim the stems, and refill the vase with fresh water. If the bouquet is now significantly smaller, consider swapping out the original vase for a smaller one.
- If you've got a candle here, trim the too-long wick with scissors or just pinch it off with your fingers, and light it.
- Now pour a glass of wine or a tall iced tea, and relax while you wait. Cheers!

The Ten-Minute Clean: Entryway

Got ten minutes or, more likely, five? That's all you need to make your entryway shine. In fact, your foyer can get by week after week, if need be, with this speedy approach. This quick clean is easy-peasy pecan pie. Plus, if you're pressed for time, it's nice to have a list to follow:

- First, set aside shoes, coats, and the rug to prevent dust from land-ing on them.

- Next, spray a microfiber cloth or old newspaper with a 50/50 vinegar-water solution, and wipe down your mirror and/or any glass-framed artwork. And dust any items on your entryway table plus the table itself. Everything will look instantly better!
- Sweep or vacuum the floor, and shake out the rug outdoors or over a trash can before returning it to the space, along with the shoes and coats.
- If you've got a bouquet, throw out any dead flowers and refill the vase with fresh water.
- Done! Look at that—you've got an extra three or so minutes. No, don't start cleaning another room. It's time to pour a glass of wine. *Salut!*

Adding That Element of Fun

As Julie Andrews recommended in *Mary Poppins*, adding fun to your chores is key. For me, I find the fun with ten-minute (or less) cleaning playlists I make (with help from my partner, Ross) for every room in the house. Maybe you'd rather listen to an audiobook or podcast. You do you. But if music moves you, feel free to crank my playlists.

Or make your own: Keep each list to a few songs, roughly equaling ten minutes. Over time, I begin to know, for example, that I should be dusting by the beginning of "Just Can't Get Enough." And by the time "You Spin Me Round" wraps, snap—as Mary Poppins would say—I'm done.

My Ten-Minute Cleaning Playlist: Entryway (upbeat)
- "Break My Stride" by Matthew Wilder (3:00)
- "Just Can't Get Enough" by Depeche Mode (3:40)
- "You Spin Me Round (Like a Record)" by Dead or Alive (3:19)

My Ten-Minute Cleaning Playlist: Entryway (mellow)
- "Holding Back the Years" by Simply Red (4:29)
- "You're the Best Thing" by the Style Council (5:40)

CHEAP FRILLS

I remember a beautiful winter day back in college. The snow was falling and I was meandering my way back home. Along the way I found a downed magnolia branch, at least four feet long, that was practically architectural.

No matter that my apartment was still blocks away—I was determined to drag the branch home, making an artistic path through the snow. Once home, I found just the right container: a heavy old garden pot decorated with painted lichen and glazed on the inside. I filled it with water and plunked the branch in, knowing that as long as the dormant branch had water, it would last for weeks. Placed on a table, the pot enabled the massive branch to lean against the wall. I knew it would be striking, but I hadn't realized how beautiful its glossy green leaves would look in candlelight. It's a fond memory still.

Bouquets aren't the only flowers you can use to decorate your entryway. And your choice doesn't need to be expensive. Consider bringing home branches or leaves discovered on a woodsy walk or clipped from shrubs right outside your back door. Doing so costs nothing, brings the outdoors inside, and changes the energy in any room, especially an entryway. What could be more welcoming right inside your front door?

CHAPTER 2

LIVING SPACE
BECOME A LIVING (ROOM) LEGEND

Housework can't kill you, but why take the chance?

—Phyllis Diller

Fear not as you make your home your own.

If you take one key message from this book, this is it. Why? Because it's so easy to feel intimidated, overwhelmed, even paralyzed by the thought of selecting a sofa, choosing a paint color, or even buying throw pillows. But fear won't get you anywhere. And these decisions should be fun, not scary.

Fears might bubble up, especially when it's time to start refreshing your living room—or parlor, den, or multifunctional room—a room that you and your loved ones plus visitors enjoy.

Too often people watch home décor shows, page through shelter magazines, or scroll through opulent home shots online and throw up their hands, feeling sure their spaces are "less than." You might ask: How could I even begin to make my house look that good? That question has you losing from the get-go. Instead, stop playing the comparison game and ask: How can I make my space my own? Or how can I make my space inviting, relaxing, warm, and cozy for everyone who uses it?

When flipping through home images, we often get to see the "before" shot—you know the one, that photo snapped by a homeowner, with little attention to lighting or styling. In fact, the worse it looks, the more astounding the transformation appears.

And then our eyes land on the marvelous "after" shots—those drop-dead-gorgeous reveals we aspire to. But I'd argue that we're thinking about those "after photos" all wrong. Just like models photoshopped to kingdom come, those shots don't reflect reality.

What we don't see are the hours and hours of work that go into them: the culling of the space, perhaps removing a chair or two or adjusting the ottoman for better angles; the thoughtful styling of the bookshelves and shelf accessories; the careful editing of the objects on the coffee table; and the meticulous selection of flowers for the ultimate oh-so-casual bouquet. Believe me: If you had a team of pros prepping your space for a photo shoot, it would look amazing too.

I'd love to see the real "after" shot—the one with the new living room plus a mug or two forgotten on the marble sofa table, crumbs on the silk dupioni couch (I could totally clean that), TV remotes under the nesting side tables, socks on the cherry hardwood floor, a crumpled newspaper on the upholstered club chair, and perhaps even a laundry basket of folded (fingers crossed) clothes plunked down right in the middle. Now that room is living.

I've said it before and I'll say it again: Don't be afraid—whether you're living large or living on a shoestring, you can make the living room your own.

Getting Inspired

The great architect Sarah Susanka, known for her Not So Big House philosophy, says, "In the same way that music inspires us to certain feelings, space can do the same thing." And you don't need to be an interior designer or have ten thousand square feet to sing that song. As I mentioned earlier, my dad was a builder and built many grand homes, but two that stand out were not more than two thousand square feet each. I got to know these houses well, because my family and the families who lived there were friends, and I enjoyed these spaces every time we visited.

One was a farmhouse whose living room extended from the front of the residence to the back on the right side of the house. The room was split into three separate areas, cleverly divided by the homeowners with furniture and small rugs that flowed and complemented each section. Family members and visitors all hung out together in this living room, each doing their own thing or doing something together, like playing board games, watching a tennis match on TV, or just chatting in front of the fireplace.

The second house was an A-frame with an incredible deck and surrounded by woods. This home's living room featured minimal furniture: the first sectional I ever saw, an Arco metallic lamp with its signature swoop over the sofa, and a freestanding Finnish fireplace. Despite the two-story ceiling overhead, the room felt intimate and inviting.

As the old saying goes, size doesn't matter. Moreover, when you have unlimited square footage, it's easy to create a remarkable design. You have to be clever to do that with a smaller house, and these two homes delivered clever in spades.

What does your living room offer right now? What attributes do you love? What's just okay? And what do you dislike or even hate? With a small budget, you can still make changes—you only need to give yourself permission. That's true for me whether I'm washing a dry-clean-only sweater or refreshing a space in my home. Cut yourself some slack. Remember: Those too-good-to-be-true images are just that. Your spaces are real.

Consider these three questions:

1. Is your living space, well, livable? How could you amp up its livability?
2. How might you make your space more . . . homey, feminine, masculine, lovely, whimsical, or Zen? What word or words suit you best?
3. Most important, does your space function for you and the people who regularly enjoy it?

Usually it takes a long time to make a home your own—in fact, for most of us, it's an ongoing process. What works for a single person or a couple today needs adjusting when a child or an aging parent joins the household. As children grow up, spaces might need to mature too—maybe a drum set takes the place of the toy bin, or beanbag chairs (perfect for gaming) are added to the living room layout. Change is often good—and required to make living easier and more fun.

Time to Freshen Up

Change was on our minds when Ross and I road-tripped to Duluth, Minnesota, shortly after we bought our 1883 brownstone. We were there to visit the Glensheen Mansion.

From early childhood, I've loved visiting historic homes—our family toured them wherever we traveled, including the late-nineteenth-century Biltmore Estate, a 175,000-square-foot French Renaissance chateau in Asheville, North Carolina; Monticello, designed by Thomas Jefferson and built by enslaved people beginning in the 1770s near Charlottesville, Virginia; and the Moraine Farm, a 46,000-square-foot home built in 1912, complete with observatory and indoor fountain (I still want one), in Dayton, Ohio. Their historic nature, their architecture, and their interior design enthralled me.

Glensheen, as it's known, is a thirty-nine-room, 20,000-square-foot mansion built at the turn of the last century by the Congdon family, who helped introduce iron mining in northern Minnesota. Today, the estate remains intact, right down to its century-old sheets in the linen closet. (Two murders also took place in this home, including one with a candlestick—yep, just like in the game Clue—in 1977. But that's a story for another book.)

The reason Ross and I visited Glensheen was to be inspired by this stately home built during our brownstone's era and featuring the same core aesthetic. What our tour revealed in every room was sheer splendor—opulent painting, plastering, wallpapering, glazing, woodworking, flooring, and more. What we took away were lots of ideas, including light fixtures to order for our foyer; push-button light switches, which I still plan to add; the need for walnut floors (we dyed our second-floor maple floors a deep walnut); rich, dark carpeting, plus carpeted stairs (which we added—check and check); the notion that items must be both functional and decorative; plus furniture arrangements and scale.

CALLED ON THE CARPET

Yes, you can clean your carpets at home. It costs basically nothing but some sweat equity. To clean a small throw rug, you can simply toss it into the washing machine and then hang it to dry.

To clean a large rug is a different story. If you're enjoying warm weather, take your rug outside and place it faceup on a clean driveway or large clean sheet. Spray the top of your rug with a yard hose (not a power washer), sprinkle soap flakes on it, and rub the soap in with your fingers. (If your rug is eight by ten feet or larger, this will take some time.) Then rinse it off. Now flip the rug over and spray the back. Flip it back over again and let the rug dry outdoors.

If you're one of those lucky people who experiences snow firsthand, wait for a fresh snowfall. Then take your area rug outside and place it faceup on an area of snow for five minutes to chill slightly. Next, flip the rug upside down on a clean patch of snow for twenty minutes. Then, flip it back over and, with a stiff corn or straw broom, sweep snow onto the top of the rug and let sit that way for another twenty minutes. Now sweep off the snow and let it warm up in your kitchen or garage before returning it to the living room.

But let's say you have no snow, and even if you did, your rug is really too large to haul outside anyway. If that's the case, here's my trick: First, vacuum the entire rug. Next, fold the rug in half and vacuum the half of the rug, aka the backing, that's now facing up. Then unfold the rug and fold over the other side. Now vacuum that side of the backing. Easy!

What home—either online or in person—might inspire you and your living room refresh? Historic home tours are available across the country, in large cities and small towns. You might sign up for an architectural tour of a neighborhood, visit open houses, watch *Architectural Digest* tours of celebrity homes online, spend time on Zillow, or just pore over design magazines. You never know where inspiration might come.

New York State of Mind

Next, Ross and I got to work, incorporating these ideas plus many others into our new home. New York City, one of my favorite places in the world, also proved inspirational. When NYC comes to mind, I think of Times Square, the Empire State Building, and the Chrysler Building all lit up at night—metallic and shiny, glittery and magical. That's how I wanted our house to feel, and that's why our home is designed to look its loveliest at night.

Our living room especially is at its most beautiful in the evening with its metallic silver walls (I applied a decorative finish); a 1920s Dutch brass chandelier that came with the house (we've sheathed its small bulbs with hound's-tooth lampshades and hung an orange-and-green tassel from its center); lacquered furniture; lots of lamps; and a decorative mirror. Finally, both the living room and the adjoining den (formerly the dining room) feature chocolate-brown couches (tweed and leather respectively). At night we relax on one of the couches, read books or watch TV, often wrapped up in any of the myriad blankets we keep handy (it's Minnesota after all), and enjoy the twinkling lights all around.

Like Glensheen and NYC, other design pairings might mix Miami's Art Deco colors of pink and gray with the low, kickback furniture and dramatic up-lighting often found in desert homes. Or perhaps British furnishings are layered with LA cool—for example, displaying an English rose tea set on a Lucite table. You get the idea. A stylish jumble can be fun, injecting life into your space and showing off your personal panache.

What city, state, or country might inspire your living room refresh? Perhaps your hometown if you now live far away? The city you live in right now? The place your ancestors emigrated from? A favorite vacation destination? One friend of mine is head over heels in love with Venice. So she's featured decorative objects and artworks from the City of Water throughout her house.

Now that you've thought about homes and places that might influence the look of your living room, let's consider the items that actually make up a living space.

Giving it a light touch. Besides natural light from windows, three types of lighting illuminate any room: ambient (or general) lighting, task lighting, and accent lighting.

That's true in every room of your house. Additionally, placing lamps at varying levels creates a homey and more interesting space. Take a peek at your living room and count up the lights, noting their positions. Go ahead—I'll wait. Are you surprised by how few or how many you have? Are they all on one level or are they at varying heights?

Our living room shines thanks to more than a dozen lights: the aforementioned brass chandelier, a small black lacquer lamp with a green silk shade sitting atop a storage basket, a decorative light with lots of tiny light bulbs next to our hutch, a simple little lamp plus a pink salt lamp on our bookshelf, wax candles and electrified candles on our mantel, two tiny lamps with prisms, a wall sconce, and—the pièce de résistance—a Statue of Liberty light on my rolltop desk. Oh, and there's the wood-burning fireplace, which we sometimes light; a tall floor lamp tucked away in a corner; and a big glass bubble light, very 1970s, next to my desk.

Like I said, the room features lots of lights—a great trick to make a room both attractive and inviting. A second trick: using 7-watt light bulbs. They're in practically every lamp in our living room except for

WHEN SPOT MAKES A SPOT

It happens. So what's a dog owner to do to clean the carpet?

- If it's feces, remove as much as possible and then spray the area with a 50/50 vinegar-water solution. Now scrub the area with laundry soap and a brush. Now to sterilize, mix 1 tablespoon of sodium percarbonate, also called oxygen bleach, in 1 quart warm water. Next, soak a clean towel in the solution and press down on the affected area; then fold and flip the towel as it soaks up any last traces of feces, always using a clean section of the towel to absorb more. Finally, if needed, re-treat the stained area and blot again with a clean towel freshly soaked in the solution. Once the stain is gone, to stop all that cleaning power, apply a fresh towel wetted down with water only. Then blot the area with a dry towel.

- If it's urine, mix 1 tablespoon sodium percarbonate, also called oxygen bleach, in 1 quart warm water. Next, soak a clean towel in the solution and press down on the affected area; then fold and flip the towel and press again, always using a clean section of the towel. Continue doing this until you've used every part of the cloth and the scent of urine is gone. Then, to stop all that cleaning power, apply a fresh towel wetted down with water only. Then blot the area with a dry towel. If you've taken all these steps and there's still a definite urine scent, use a steam cleaner and a solution of 2 table-spoons sodium percarbonate and 1 quart warm water.

the lamps we read by. Think about upscale restaurants: They don't use overhead lighting in the evenings. Instead, lights are dimmed, and often a candle glows on every table. At night, do you want to relax in a living space with bright lights overhead? Or do you want a softly lit room? My point exactly. Why not mimic that look in your own living space?

Speaking of light bulbs, LED light bulbs let you use whatever wattage you want in practically any lamp. That's thanks to their greatly reduced ambient heat compared to incandescent lighting. You can also tailor the color of your light bulbs—choose soft white (surprisingly, the warmest of the bulbs), warm white, cool white, and daylight (almost blue light). Light bulbs are rated on the Kelvin scale, which measures the bulb's color temperature. The higher the number, the cooler the bulb. I'd suggest warmer bulbs for a living room, especially one used mostly at night. You can also select colorful bulbs like pink, red, orange, yellow, blue, and green. While you may not want to use them every day, a single pink light bulb in one lamp might offer a fun pop of color on a bookshelf or sofa table. Or swap your standard light bulbs for colorful bulbs for a party. You might also consider Edison bulbs; these reproductions look like Thomas Edison's originals; they come in myriad shapes and sizes and offer a warm glow.

Personalizing the art. As you've guessed by now, I'm a "more is more" guy. What I'm not is an "art for art's sake" guy. Minimalist or maximalist, art should be personal, reflect you and your likes, and cost just what you can afford. Even the idea of art—what is art?!—should be up to you.

That's certainly true of the art in our living room. We have a striking woodprint that cost more than a couple of pennies. But we also have a mirror framed with what looks like twigs over our fireplace, a New York City souvenir plate, a decoupage plate, a framed postcard, and a framed DVD cover.

Lots of people select artwork to match their furniture, but that's not a rule. Honestly, nothing hung in our living room was chosen because it matches our couch, chairs, or desk. Our art reflects our wide-ranging interests, is often sentimental, and simply matters to one or both of us.

Art should make you happy. That's according to me and according to science. Even better, art improves our health and well-being, say psychologists Stefano Mastandrea, Sabrina Fagioli, and Valeria Biasi ("Art and Psychological Well-Being: Linking the Brain to the Aesthetic Emotion," *Frontiers in Psychology*, April 4, 2019). Indeed! Why hang someone else's idea of great art in your house? Show off what you love, whether that's a landscape oil painting, a Buddha sculpture, your kid's art, a poster of your favorite soccer team, or a print of cats playing Parcheesi.

Additionally, framing and hanging your own photos or even blowing them up to poster size can lift your mood. Happiness expert Gretchen Rubin says, "One of the best ways to make yourself happy in the present is to recall happy times from the past. Photos are a great memory prompt." That family wedding on the beach? That stunning

HL Tip: Ensure that you and your companions are breathing the cleanest possible air. That's true whether you own your home or you're renting. In fact, if you're renting, it's likely your landlord is not buying top-of-the-line filters for your heat and/or AC. So swap out the provided filters with the best ones you can afford. It's a game changer, especially for those who have allergies, live in a household with three or more people, and/or have pets. If you've got pets, consider buying high-efficiency particulate air (HEPA) filters, which can trap up to 99.97 percent of airborne particles. And be sure to change your filters at least every three months, increasing their efficiency and saving money on your utility costs in the long run.

hike you took in Acadia? That once-in-a-lifetime trip to Italy? Get those photos on the wall and be reminded of precious memories every time you walk into the room.

Taking that idea a step further, a friend of mine bought a digital picture frame for her father and then invited the extended family to email him photos that automatically populate in the frame. Now new images pop up constantly in his den, reminding him of the people and places he loves. Plus, he knows family members are thinking of him every time they hit send.

Here's one more compelling reason to personalize your art: I believe the greater the variety of art, the higher the room's chic quotient. Framed matchbooks, an estate-sale watercolor, a needlepoint pillow by Nana, framed vintage sheet music, or a finger-paint masterpiece by your toddler—it all belongs.

Not long ago, someone asked what I'd do if I had too much art. Like if I ran out of wall space? What a question! I'd simply hang it from floor to ceiling like in the Louvre (if it's good enough for them . . .).

Setting the mood with paint. Dozens of online articles offer advice about choosing living room colors, including "21 Best Living Room Paint Colors, According to Designers," "40 Best Living Room Paint Color Ideas," and even "80 Living Room Paint Color Ideas." What do these titles tell us? That you can paint your living room any color you

HL Tip: If your home has more than one level, a stair basket is a great solution for returning items to their proper places. Designed to sit on two steps at a time, this basket is the perfect place to stash an item whenever you find something that belongs upstairs. The next time you take the stairs, grab those items—or the whole basket—and carry them with you for delivery.

like. I remember accompanying Nancy to a paint store when, in one fell swoop, she bought all the paints she needed for much of her house. Of course, embracing change is just who Nancy is, but there's a lesson there: Change can make your life better, brighter, and more colorful!

It's true: Paint is an easy and cheap way to dramatically change a living space. Consider swapping neutral walls for mossy green, or flat white walls for inky blue. Or paint three walls gray and one hot pink. Change your mind in a couple of years, a month, or a week? Just paint a new color.

For my first apartment, I selected the colors of Key lime pie: The living room walls were awash in soft yellow, which flowed into the hallway. There, the chair rail divided the top of the wall, which I painted that same yellow, from the bottom of the wall, which I painted green. Hence, the Key lime pie palette. Meanwhile, the living room featured stylish dark green curtains of heavy brushed twill, which kept out noise and light when closed. And I hung them from a metal pipe, which I'd spray-painted black and added cheap arrow finials painted gold and stuck into a cork at either end of the pipe. (Fancy doesn't need to be expensive.)

Here's the truth: There's not one perfect, elusive color that's the end-all or be-all color for your living room—or any room in your home, for that matter. Just like there are lots of fish in the sea, lots of colors will look spectacular on your walls.

If you find yourself stuck choosing a color or a color palette, consider the way in which you primarily use your living room. If its primary function is serving as your day-in, day-out office, choose a paint color that sets the mood for your day and will make you happy for hours on end. If it's a lively space with lots of family members interacting at all times of the day and night, consider selecting an energetic color like orange, pink, or yellow. If it's a space used mostly for unwinding, nature-inspired colors like blue or green make a fine choice. If you plan to entertain guests, consider a refined, muted color with gray undertones, like dusty blue, soft green, or delicate pink. Once you've got a general idea of the color family you're considering, get some paint chips, a sample can of wall paint, or even a peel-and-stick sample or two, and try them out on your wall. Now choose one and commit. It's highly likely that you're going to love it in your space. And if you don't? You know what to do.

Packing a design punch with pillows. Want to transform the look of your room fast? A switcheroo of your throw pillows is often all you need—whether you do it seasonally or whenever the mood strikes.

But there's no need to buy new pillows. (Sorry, TJ Maxx.) If you're crafty, you can make pillow covers with scissors, fusible tape, or a sewing machine. Or take that vintage shirt you love but doesn't fit or your grandpa's old wool jacket to a crafty friend (along with a platter of brownies) and beg a favor.

Or if you're like me, search for pleasing pillow covers online. They come in every possible color, shape, size, and style. And the great thing about pillow covers is they're always removable, so you can wash them!

Let's say, however, that you don't own any pillows or you want to start fresh. Then begin by purchasing pillow forms, the plain or uncovered pillow shapes tucked inside pillows and found at fabric stores or online. But there are so many types—which ones should you select? If you want your pillows to look perfect and decorative, but you actually plan to throw them aside when you plunk down on your sofa, buy inexpensive foam forms. But if you want to use your couch pillows for cozying up during a movie, napping, or even propping up that sprained ankle from too much grooving while you clean, then purchase down or faux-down pillow forms.

On my sofa I use both—down inserts in our large pillows and inexpensive foam forms in our small pillows. In no particular order are our twenty-six-by-twenty-six-inch pillows: a Coogi pillow (like the Australian sweaters), a KISS album-cover pillow, a black beaded skull pillow, and a velvet pillow in a leopard print. The combo is very rock and roll. We also have two small pillows—a lumbar cushion in a cover I made from scraps of one fabric in three colorways and a tiny orange-and-brown cashmere pillow that says *CHIC*. I saw the latter at a department store and had to have it because I thought it was so ridiculous.

Against our traditional camelback sofa, our pillows are hilariously subversive. They're our personality and design style—what I like to call "Andy Warhol at Monticello."

Who's your design style? Cher meets Frank Lloyd Wright (bright, beaded accessories in a sea of handsome wood furniture)? A neutral Harry Styles (bold natural prints—e.g., kiwi, sunflowers, watermelon—in grays, blacks, and whites)? Or perhaps Diana Ross at the beach (bold colorways and accessories against a sea of blue)? Determining your signature style in celebrity parlance can be fun and help hone your spaces and home purchases.

Spacing out. Keeping storage on display is the trick to maximizing living room square footage. For example, a decorative basket under my hutch is filled with extra candles and coasters, while a throw on top hides everything underneath. A few decorative boxes on my book-cases store small items I don't need out all the time. I also keep things tucked inside my desk and under a skirted table. Meanwhile, vases and bowls serve as decorative objects on our bookshelves most of the time, but they're within reach when needed. I've also placed a white platter on the top of my desk; it makes a great backdrop for my architecture souvenir buildings, but it's ready in a moment for serving.

Where might you find storage? Flat containers under your sofa can store photo albums, back issues of favorite magazines, or your latest knitting project. Assign each end table a function, like storing candles in one and vases in another. Some ottomans offer secret storage for blankets or games. And, of course, baskets come in all shapes and sizes and add visual interest as well as storage.

Allowing for flexibility. If your living room wears many hats, in-cluding homework hangout, binge-watching space, frequent dining room, yoga studio, and more, congratulations! You're making the most of that room. A friend told me about her elderly neighbor's comment when he dropped by to check on her. She apologized for the laundry stacked in piles around the living room. "No apologies necessary," he said. "Today, your living room is your laundry room." I love that. It's your house and it should serve you, not the other way around.

In my first smidge of an apartment, I had to get creative to make my furniture multipurpose. Sometimes I used my drop-leaf table (whose leaves folded down to save space) as a console table, placing it against a wall and topping it with a lamp and some decorative items. Other times, when friends came to dinner, I pulled it out from the wall, flipped up the drop leaves, and set it as our dining room table. That's the thing about living room furniture—it can flex.

You can also move furniture around to serve your needs. Recently a friend bought a large sectional and asked me how I'd suggest maximizing seating for party guests. Usually, the couch's L is on one side, but together we moved it to the center of the couch so people could sit back-to-back for extra seating. Don't be afraid to rearrange your furniture—just for one night or for a whole new look.

Addressing the elephant in the room: the television. In decades past, hiding your TV inside an armoire was de rigueur. And if you still love to close up that cabinet at the end of the night, that's great. But a flat-screen television doesn't need to hide. Place it where it makes the most sense. Just don't hang it over a working fireplace, where it would be exposed to heat.

You also don't need to have every furniture item pointed at the TV like pews in a church. You can swivel furniture to face the screen whenever needed. Or maybe you don't even have a TV—after all, you can stream programs on your phone or tablet. Or do as a friend of mine does and use a projector. Whenever he wants to watch a show, he simply points the projector at the wall.

Here are a few more TV ideas: Hosting a party? In the background, play a fun movie that complements your theme. Don't have a fireplace? During the holidays, flick on that video of a roaring fire. And at an anniversary or birthday party, link your phone to the TV and play a slideshow featuring the guest(s) of honor.

A DOZEN MORE REFRESHES

1. Make or buy slipcovers for your chairs to give your room a whole new look—shabby chic or just plain chic. You can even cover a chair or two with simple sheets, tucking them in around the cushions and adding throw pillows. (This is also a great and inexpensive way to try out a new color.)

2. Rather than buy a bunch of throws, invest in one luxurious blanket—color-blocked and cashmere, leather trimmed, or monogrammed—for a major style upgrade.

3. Layer a plush and fluffy sheepskin on a chair or sofa for a posh and cozy look. (Sheepskins are byproducts of meat production—sheep aren't raised for their skins.)

4. Dress up an armoire, a piece of art, or a window with a pom-pom tassel or a miniature flag bunting. This kind of layering can make a huge difference to your room's hominess factor.

5. Add a splash of color to your room by painting flowers, hearts, or a wreath on a window with tempera paint. Beforehand, mix the paint with laundry soap flakes (not detergent!) for easy removal.

6. Make over your accessories—lamps, candlesticks, or baskets you already own or new thrift store finds—with spray paint. It comes in every color of the rainbow and myriad textures, including satin, matte, stone, flat, and more.

7. Attach a loop of grosgrain ribbon—a strong, tightly woven fabric—to the top of framed artwork for visual interest and a bit of trickery; the picture will look like it's hanging from the ribbon.

8. Frame a rectangle of amazing wallpaper in a poster frame for an inexpensive, fun piece of art. Or use a trio of poster frames and three wallpaper rectangles in the same color palette or by the same artist for a focal wall.

9. Swap out small accessories, throw pillows, and/or blankets for a fresh look every season. For example, every summer a friend of mine leans her tiny, seated doll, wearing a 1920s swimsuit, on the edge of a potted plant.

10. Cover the inside of a lampshade with peel-and-stick wallpaper. Or spray the shade's interior with a metallic paint.

11. Paint a rummage sale dresser with chalkboard paint and then keep a bowl of colorful chalk handy for daily or weekly messages.

12. Hang a disco ball in your living room. What—you already have one in your laundry room, you say? You can never have too many!

Before turning our attention to cleaning, let's sum everything up: First, don't be afraid to make decisions—about color, wallpaper, furniture, or accessories. It's your house. Remember: You can always make a new decision—it's okay to change your mind. Second, your home should feature items that bring joy to you and anyone who lives with you—your loved ones! In other words, don't settle for an okay lamp from a discount store when you might have looked a bit longer and found one you really loved at a yard sale. Third, all those images online and in magazines don't reflect real life. Don't feel intimidated by over-the-top photos of opulent homes. You too can style your house for a party, but you can't live like that every day. Go easy on yourself and enjoy your space. Finally, you don't need a lot to make a living room: a gallon of paint, an understanding of the items that make you happy, a plant or two, and a really great estate sale find can make your room look just as fabulous as if you had all the money in the world. Sometimes it looks even better.

Time to Clean Up

Your living space undoubtedly sees a lot of activity. So it's likely to need a full cleaning once a week or at least once every two weeks. If you've got guests coming over soon, you might clean a day or two before. But even if you never entertain, it's just as important to clean the space for you and anyone who lives with you. You deserve a lovely space to enjoy. And like pulling on your favorite jeans after they've been freshly washed and dried, walking into your living space after it's been cleaned makes the room that much more enjoyable. Let's get started.

- When you're making the most of your living space, random items tend to collect there. Gather up what doesn't belong—yesterday's coffee cups, the random magazine, a homework assignment, days-old newspapers, the stray sock, etc. My trick: I pack them up in a designated tote bag; then I carry it around the house, delivering each item to wherever it belongs.

- Next, wipe away any cobwebs gathering in your ceiling's corners with a wool duster, and brush off all your light fixtures—ceiling and otherwise, including cloth shades—with a horsehair brush. (Be sure your lights are off when dusting.) Check to see if all your light bulbs are working; replace any that are on the blink.

- Now it's time to dust. Simply dampen a microfiber cloth and get to work. I know people who hate dusting, but I can't view it that way. When dusting my desk, my lamps, or my collection of miniature souvenir buildings (the Empire State Building, the Minneapolis skyline, and the Eiffel Tower, among them), there's something about the process that pays respect to these items. I'm taking care of objects that are important to me. If the things you're dusting aren't important to you anymore, maybe it's time to donate.

- Next, spray the 50/50 vinegar-water solution on a microfiber cloth or newspaper to wipe down glass-fronted art and windows. (The solution should wipe away fingerprints and paw prints with ease.)

- Remove the throw pillows and cushions from your chairs and sofa, pocket any loose change, stick the pencils and pens back in the kitchen junk drawer, and vacuum up the crumbs and popcorn with a handheld vacuum or an attachment on your regular vacuum.

- Return the cushions to the furniture. Now flip each throw pillow upside down and fluff; then return them to the couch. Refold any blankets and drape them over the arm or back of the sofa or place in a basket. Now give your upholstered couch and chairs a light spray with vodka to remove any unwanted scents. Or, if it's been a while, consider removing and washing the pillow covers and the throws. By the time you're done cleaning, you'll likely be hanging them up to dry.

- As for the upholstered cushions, remove any spots quickly and easily with a horsehair brush and laundry soap. And once every

CHEERS TO WINE SPILLS

Did you or a guest spill red wine on your carpet? No worries—just pour another glass. Then later that night, the next morning, or even a couple of days later, you can remove that organic stain quickly and easily. Truly.

Mix 1 tablespoon of sodium percarbonate, also called oxygen bleach, in 1 quart warm water and add to a carpet cleaner/extractor. Now put that machine to work.

Don't have a carpet cleaner/extractor? Then soak a clean towel in the solution and press down on the stain; then fold and flip the towel as it soaks up the stain, always using a clean section of the towel to absorb more. Finally, if needed, re-treat the stained area and blot again with a clean towel freshly soaked in the solution.

Once the stain is gone, to stop all that cleaning power, apply a fresh towel wetted down with water only. Then blot the area with a dry towel.

Did the wine also land on a garment? Simply dip the stained portion of the item into the solution, give it a swish— the stain should change color—and throw it in the wash. Easy.

couple of months, unzip the chair and sofa cushion covers and remove the sofa cover (if possible) and wash. When they're damp, right out of the wash, replace them on the cushions and the sofa, and stand to dry. Machine-drying may cause shrinkage and make zipping them back onto the cushions difficult.

- If you've got a small area rug, roll it up and shake it out in your garbage can or outdoors. Before replacing it, sweep the floor with a broom or vacuum. If you've got a large area rug, simply vacuum. (To actually clean your small or large rug, see "Called on the Carpet," on page 21.)

- If you've got a laminate floor, give it a sweep with a stiff corn or straw broom. If your floor is hardwood, use a horsehair broom, which is much softer. If your sealed hardwood floor could use more than a quick sweep and you've got a steam cleaner, use that multitasker to disinfect, sanitize, degrease, deodorize, and clean your sealed floor. Now stand back in amazement to admire your handiwork. (Don't use a steam cleaner on an unsealed wood floor or an engineered floor; a steam cleaner can damage both types.)

- If you've got wall-to-wall carpet or a large area rug, grab your vacuum. Be sure to first scan the carpet for coins, hair clips, etc., to pick up before vacuuming. Also, I highly recommend leveraging all those tools that came with your vacuum. My favorite is the crevice tool that concentrates the power of your vacuum to suck up dust and dirt from any place, including room corners, ceiling corners, sofa cushions, bookcases, you name it. It's so satisfying! Plus, you can set your vacuum in the middle of the room and use the long tube attachment to reach practically anywhere. I also like the brush attachment, which I use to remove lint from my woodwork and pleated lampshades. Making vacuuming your final cleaning step almost feels like graduation. You're finished! Now you can slowly back out of the room, vacuum in hand, as the strains of "Pomp and Circumstance" play.

- Throw your cap in the air, Mary. You've made it after all.

The Ten-Minute Clean: Living Space

Your in-laws, your boss, or—oh no!—Simon Cowell (or someone equally judgy) is coming over (or you can pretend they are)—and time has gotten away from you. Not to worry! It's time to scurryfunge—an old-timey word that means to quickly tidy up the room before guests arrive. Here's how to clean your living room in a flash.

- Pack up anything that doesn't belong in this room in your designated tote bag or in a laundry basket, and set it aside until later. Or tuck these items away in your favorite stash-away spot—a spare bedroom or perhaps under the couch? To paraphrase Julia Child, "Only God sees under the sofa."
- Now it's time to dust. Generally, there's no need to lift every lamp or knickknack. If you can write your name in the dust, just wipe away with a soft cloth and you're done. However, if you can write the Declaration of Independence, it's time for something stronger: Grab your feather duster or a damp microfiber cloth and get busy.
- Sweep and/or vacuum the space. It doesn't need to be perfect, just clean enough that the vacuum lines look like you made an effort.
- Plump the pillows and drape that refolded throw in your favorite spot.
- Straighten everything on the coffee table and turn on your lamps (which you've also dusted).
- Set out a bowl of snacks, pour yourself a cup of tea (or a glass of wine), and await your guests' arrival.

My Ten-Minute Cleaning Playlist: Living Space (Upbeat)
- "Strike It Up" by Black Box (4:58)
- "Vogue" by Madonna (4:49)

My Ten-Minute Cleaning Playlist: Living Space (Mellow)
- "Our House" by Crosby, Stills, Nash & Young (3:02)
- "Any Place I Hang My Hat Is Home" by Barbra Streisand (2:43)
- "Home" by Diana Ross from *The Wiz* (4:02)

INCREASING YOUR HOME'S IQ

Consider how you can simplify your life with more technology. My baseline? Being able to control everything in my home when I'm halfway around the world, visiting a cashmere goat farm in Italy. (A guy can dream.) Everything? Sure! You've likely already got a programmable thermostat that can be accessed via your phone. Where do you go from there? Well, you no longer need timers on your lights during the holidays or vacation. Simply connect your lights to smart plugs and then control them via a phone app. How lovely to be able to flick on the lights from afar and have them glowing as you reach your front door late at night. Or to be able to turn off all the lights as you're falling asleep without ever getting out of bed.

What else can you control with your phone? Your security system, your smart video doorbell, and your radon and smoke detectors. You might also consider adding smart appliances to your home. Often programmed and controlled via Wi-Fi, these include small appliances like blenders, coffee makers, irons, microwaves, and vacuums, and large appliances like refrigerators, washers, and dryers (swoon). Many also follow voice commands and offer touch screens.

Bonus: If you ever move, you can take all of these things with you—except for the thermostat. My home's latest and greatest smart home purchase is an HVAC system that accommodates various heating and cooling settings for different rooms in our house. Being comfortable is important!

HOW COZY IS YOUR LIVING ROOM?

Candles are lit and glowing. Blankets are within reach from anywhere in the room. Feet are propped on a pillow. A mug of hot chocolate, dark and sweet, is at your elbow. Ah, the joy of coziness. In my adulthood, being cozy is something I've really warmed up to. I especially have come to appreciate blankets. Minnesota's winters and ever-fluctuating weather year-round demand a good throw or two or ten. (Or a king-size electric blanket, for that matter.) How cozy is your living room? See how it rates, from 10 (the absolute coziest—think: kittens-wrapped-in-a-blanket cozy) to 1 (not cozy at all—think: porcupine).

10 People are so relaxed in your space that they fall asleep on your couch. And drool.

9 "Come as you are"—that's your motto, whether guests are dressed to the nines, outfitted in athleisure, or clothed in footed jammies.

8 You've got so many guests your house is often mistaken for a hotel.

7 Friends know they can drop by whenever—you've always got candles, throws, and loads of snacks at the ready.

6 Game night? Everyone wants to play when you're hosting.

5 Your fireplace is ready—at the flip of a switch.

4 You happily offer visitors Hi-C and a plate of crackers.

3 Your thermostat tops out at 67°F—guests know to bring extra socks and sweaters.

2 Your concrete floor, straight-back chairs, and fluorescent lighting really make a statement.

1 Your last visit to Alcatraz prompted a revamp.

CHAPTER 3

DINING ROOM
EAT, DRINK, AND BE MERRIER

One cannot think well, love well, sleep well,
if one has not dined well.

—Virginia Woolf, *A Room of One's Own*

Have you got a room in your house you never use? I didn't think so. Few of us do. Most rooms these days pull double, triple, even quadruple duty—transforming in a single day, for example, from bedroom to office to yoga studio. But if you grew up in the 1960s or '70s, you might remember a dining room or living room that was barely used and generally off limits, especially to kids.

Or raise your hand if you had a friend whose upholstered furniture was covered in thick, clear plastic. Yes, I see you and you and, yes, you in the back there. Me too. For those of you not in the know, that plastic wasn't removed when guests came over. Oh, no. That plastic stayed on the furniture 24/7/365, and guests sat on it. Imagine how that felt in summer, in shorts. Sticky, sticky. (Eek! You shouldn't be able to clean your couch with spray cleaner.)

While my family had no plastic-covered furniture, my childhood dining room was reserved for adult visitors and holiday use only. Our immediate family rarely ate in the dining room, say, on a random Tuesday. In fact, we so rarely ever entered the dining room that we could've done a weekly ten-minute clean practically year-round.

Looking back, my strongest dining room memory isn't even eating there but helping myself to cookies. The weeks between Thanksgiving and Christmas were the time of year when my mom baked the most. Generally, my brother, Jarrod, and I ate carrots, apples, pretzels, and other healthy snacks my mom provided. But during the holidays, she transformed our kitchen into a bakery and our dining room into its glass case.

There we'd find small plates and napkins stacked next to Mom's collection of vintage 1940s tins packed with her homemade treats: chocolate chip cookies, nut balls (her favorites), sugar cookies (my favorites), cutout cookies, no-bake cookies, paper-thin Spanish lace cookies, and slice-and-bake cookies called Santa's whiskers (recipes for many of these begin on page 207). And then there was her homemade cinnamon candy (which she'd let me hit with a hammer to break into pieces) and the fudges—chocolate, peanut butter, and sour cream walnut.

We never actually ate these treats in the dining room. Instead, we'd balance our little plates as we walked through the kitchen, past the breakfast area, and then up the stairs to the TV room. I remember noshing on Christmas cookies in front of holiday shows like *Frosty the Snowman, A Charlie Brown Christmas,* and *The Homecoming,* the film that introduced us to the Waltons (I still dearly love that movie). I also recall delivering cookie platters to friends and family on Christmas Eve.

Today, I not only don't have a formal dining room, but I also don't even have a dining room. That's because we've converted ours into a den.

Do you have a dining room and, if so, is it only used for dining? Perhaps it's transformed into an office (or two)—and is only sometimes used for dining. Or maybe your dining room is now a kid's bedroom or guest bedroom. When a friend's father-in-law was in hospice, the dining room became his bedroom, which allowed easy access to the kitchen and bathroom. I also know a couple of people whose childhood bedrooms were former dining rooms, with pocket doors and access to the kitchen for late-night snacks. Not too shabby.

These days when Ross and I entertain, everyone hangs out in the kitchen, takes dinner plates out onto our deck, or dines in the foyer. Yep—sometimes we eat in our foyer: Our hall table morphs into a din-

HL Tip: Do you display all-white dinnerware in your china cabinet? Cool! Then you can choose whatever paint or paper you desire, even—and I'd recommend this—a multicolored pattern that includes one color from your walls, or a textured paper that grabs attention.

HL Tip: If your china cabinet doesn't include built-in lighting, add battery-operated fairy lights or tea lights on one or more of the shelves to create a bit of ambience when entertaining.

ing room table with a leaf I store under my bed. And we set all the armless upholstered chairs, usually scattered all over our house, around the table. Plus, the foyer light hangs directly over our table—in fact, I chose the ceiling light location especially for this purpose.

We also, from time to time, eat in our living room. Sometimes it's just the two of us eating at our tallish round coffee table next to the fireplace. Sometimes it's four of us, with two on chairs and two on the sofa.

This is all to say that your dining room doesn't have to be a dining room. Just like ignoring those bossy fabric-care labels (which I discuss in my book *Laundry Love*), you can make your home and its spaces work for you, not the other way around. That means the original dining room can be used for any purpose you wish and your actual dining room can be wherever you choose to eat on any given day.

Where do you eat: in the kitchen, in front of the TV, on the front porch, in the den? Perhaps you might consider creating a new spot to enjoy a meal with, say, a tiny café table and chair in a corner of your bedroom, or cushions you can pull out onto your fire escape—that is, when you're not using it to dry clothes.

Time to Freshen Up

Whatever space you use for eating, you can breathe new life and a bit of fun into it. Let's imagine for the moment a dining room outfitted with a china cabinet, a buffet, and a table.

To hit the refresh button, first consider what's on display in that china cabinet. Perhaps everything has been in there since the late 1950s or at least feels like it. Then it's time to switch it up. To begin, remove everything, wipe down the display area, and clean the glass— instantly improved!

Now for the fun part: Consider the items you own that you really love. Just because it's called a china cabinet doesn't mean you have to display china. Maybe you've got a beautiful collection of black-and-white family photos, or Mexican cereal bowls, or Senegalese baskets, or sterling-silver ornaments, or first-edition novels, or hot sauce bottles. Whatever pops into mind, start there.

I'd say truly compelling china cabinets mix two or more categories of items. Consider those framed photos again. Rather than filling your cabinet with photos, I'd suggest placing pictures on the shelf closest to eye level. But don't pack them in—just use your favorites. Then, on the lowest shelf, stack plates or store your simple clear wineglasses. And on the top shelf? Place two china platters or one elegant platter and a complementary vase.

Or how about those vibrant empty hot sauce bottles? Perhaps crowd dozens on the top shelf of the cabinet and then, on the shelf below, display those multicolored Mexican cereal bowls. Finally, on the bottom shelf, stack a bunch of dishes, like Fiestaware, in a single, coordinating color. What you display should reflect you and your likes. The sky's the limit.

HL Tip: If you're entertaining, hide away a couple of extra spoons and forks, plus a serving spoon and a kitchen towel or two, in your dining room. If a guest drops an item on the floor or spills something, you'll be ready to save the day, with no embarrassment for your guest.

DOING ONE'S HOMEWORK

When Ross isn't conducting interviews or attending concerts (he's a music critic and I'm his lucky plus-one), he mostly works from home, largely in the bedroom. Meanwhile, when I'm not at my store, Mona Williams, I often work at my dining table.

We're not alone plying our trades from home. According to a McKinsey & Company 2022 report, 58 percent of Americans can work at home at least one day a week while 35 percent can work from home five days a week. And those percentages mean that millions of us have some version of a home office. If you work from home, there are lots of ways to make that space more to your liking. Let's count them down:

1. Close your eyes and imagine where you'd like to work. Maybe it's a light-filled space with a standing desk topped by a vase and matching office supplies. Or perhaps it's a fireplace-adjacent overstuffed chair where you can flip open your laptop yet be within reach of client files, tucked into a side table with drawers. Then again, some people like switching up their workspaces, enjoying a sunny kitchen in the morning and cozying up on the couch for a change of venue in the afternoon. It's your home—work where you want.

2. Next, where can you create this space? Maybe one of your kids has flown the coop, so you can revamp a bedroom. Or, if you're fresh out of rooms, consider a corner in your dining space, kitchen, or bedroom that

you can separate from the rest of the space with a sofa, room divider, or trio of plants. A closet too can be converted into an office nook; close that pocket or sliding door and your workspace is out of sight, out of mind. Some people use a similar setup in their kitchens, concealing a workspace behind kitchen cabinetry.

3. Now make a list of everything you need—it may only be a laptop and a giant coffee mug. After all, thanks to technology, few of us need multilevel inboxes, heavy-duty office desks, bookcases, and file cabinets these days. But you may require an ergonomic chair, a writing desk with a drawer or two, a rolling office supplies cart (that you can tuck away in a closet), and several outlets for all your tech gear. What items do you need to be productive?

4. Lastly, make your home office inspiring and fun. In a small space, you can be brave with color, lighting, and accessories. If it's a closet, maybe you add a cute print in removable wallpaper or that rich paint color you'd be unlikely to use anywhere else. If it's a corner in your living space, perhaps you splurge on a favorite chair, reupholster an old one, or just toss a new throw over it. Or maybe you find a task light that will bring you pleasure every time you flip the switch. Regardless of your choices, outfitting your home office exactly as you wish—perhaps differently than any other area in your home—will ensure you're creating a place you love working in.

Cooler Than Cool

I remember Ed and Fred's Desert Moon, hands down the coolest restaurant in Lexington, Kentucky, in the 1990s. It was brick, industrial, and arty, and just walking in made you feel cool yet comfortable, no matter the day—after a Friday-night movie or for Sunday brunch. It was also the first restaurant in the city that offered updated comfort food—fancy meat loaf, killer nachos, a grilled cheese to die for, and more. In truth, it gave me the confidence to serve my own souped-up grilled cheese at a dinner party. And because I'd rather impress people with my food than my tie, this was perfect for me. In truth, I'm not really a dress-for-dinner kind of guy. I may wear a tuxedo to the grocery store now and then, but I'm going to wear my jeans when you come over for dinner.

(By the way, my grilled sandwich recipe is so good that a friend requests it for his birthday every year and another friend asked to include it in a recipe booklet she handed out at her wedding. I know what you're thinking: Can I get the recipe? Yes—yes, you can; see page 211. To get your mouth watering, let me share just two ingredients: Granny Smith apples and bacon. Enough said.)

All to say, what you don't want is to create a dining space so serious or so fancy that it sucks all the fun from eating with friends and family. I remember a dinner in my twenties: I'd been invited, along with several others, to the elegant home of a friend. The dining room

HL Tip: A friend of mine keeps her stash of truffles in an old Norwegian bridal bowl inside her china cabinet. It's deep enough that her kids can't see the chocolates. What can you hide in your cabinet?

was crazy luxurious and bursting with candelabra, crystal, and Champagne. In total, it was a bit intimidating, putting the kibosh on a good time. Yes, we were enjoying our multicourse gourmet meal and the beautiful surroundings. But it wasn't until we were two wineglasses in that a guest (not me!) dared crack a joke that completely altered the mood—first with shocked silence and then riotous laughter. The juxtaposition of the oh-so-proper surroundings made the joke all the funnier.

The lesson? Don't make your dining room stuffy at the cost of a good time. Leave some room for not taking your home so seriously. Put your guests at ease and let the good times roll. As I always say, good taste is better than bad taste. But bad taste is better than no taste.

Dish It Out

Once you've decided what to display in your dining room, it's time to make those items pop. Let's say you, like my mom, own a complete dinnerware collection in blue plus matching crystal. And despite all my good ideas for changing up your display, you're sticking with the tried-and-true in your china cabinet. Fair enough. Unfortunately, the dark brown back wall of your cabinet muddies the blue tones of your lovely dishes and crystal. Do you know what might make those blue dishes pop? My favorite color: orange.

Certainly, you can paint the back wall of your china cabinet in a lively poppy, cantaloupe, or marmalade, but that's going to take some

HL Tip: Recycle those clear, simple vases that flowers are delivered in and instead keep only a few special vases that you can have out all the time—with or without flowers.

HL Tip: If you don't already have a dimmer switch in your dining room, it's high time you get one. Installing one is super easy—just watch a YouTube video, find a friend who's handy, or hire an electrician for this speedy job. A dimmer switch allows you to add instant ambience. Plus, between the wine and the dimmer, no one will know they're eating store-bought cheesecake.

prep work and might be messy. And what if you don't love the color when you're done? Instead, select peel-and-stick wallpaper and then cut it to size to fit your cabinet's back wall. Then, when you want to change your look later, simply remove the paper.

For an even cheaper but still punchy solution, find a high-quality gift wrap and use two-sided tape to adhere it to the back of your china cabinet. Or, if your cabinet was owned by Louis XIV and you don't want to mar it even with tape, cut poster board to fit the back of your cabinet and cover that with paint, peel-and-stick paper, or gift wrap. Or you might just buy a colored poster board. Whatever approach you use, a completely new look can be yours in less than two hours.

Field Day with the Buffet

Now let's turn our attention to the buffet table—by its very nature, it offers another flat surface for display. I'm going to take a quick side trip here, but stick with me: Back in college, I used to splurge on Crabtree & Evelyn toothpaste. Sure it was pricey, but it made me happy every time I used it. As a student, I certainly couldn't afford a daily latte (although like the internet, they weren't actually around back then), but I could manage to buy one fancy toothpaste

> **HL Tip:** While the dimmer switch and candles are my atmospheric go-tos, for a unique and memorable look, line up small, battery-operated lamps—perhaps interspersed with greenery—down the center of a long dining room table.

that lasted for months. In other words, just one simple indulgence brought me joy.

That, in a nutshell, is my philosophy for what to display on your sideboard or buffet. For example, maybe you love nothing more than an orange-clove-cinnamon–scented candle that transports you to Istanbul. Or maybe you like the look and color of fresh lemons—like those super-fragrant Buddha's hands that almost look like tulips—piled into a white porcelain bowl. Or maybe you fell in love with a stoneware vase you found at an estate sale that's beautiful, with or without flowers.

By purchasing fewer items, buying only those you really love—whether or not they're expensive—you're being good to yourself and the planet. After all, making your dining room look good isn't really about the furniture—it's about those flowers in your favorite vase or that cool collection of frog figurines.

Here are nine more buffet table ideas to instill more excitement in your dining room:

1. Don't have a killer table runner? Buy a fabric remnant you love, fold it lengthwise twice, iron it, and you're good to go—no sewing needed.

2. Are you a candy fiend? Collect three or five clear lidded containers, and fill each with a colorful candy.

3. Is your dining room also your office? A buffet is a perfect place to keep your cordless printer. Just figure out where to store it quickly when unexpected guests drop by.

4. For more warmth in your dining room, add a small lamp or two to your buffet. There are even buffet lamps—called, wouldn't you know it, buffet lamps—but any small lamp will do.

5. If you don't drink punch every day, plant a fern in your punch bowl and give it major real estate at the center of your buffet. (Mom, I do drink punch every day, so I'd love to have your punch bowl.)

6. A buffet offers great storage. Since it usually has deep drawers, it can serve as your butler's pantry, loaded up with all your entertaining items—from silverware and tablecloths to candles and serving platters. Or you might store a pillow and blanket for an overnight guest or reserve space for that cordless printer.

WAX OFF, WAX ON

To wax your sideboard or buffet, first buff down your table with superfine steel wool, wiping in the direction of the wood grain to remove old wax if your wax isn't self-removing. (Check your can.) Next, apply a very thin layer of clear or tinted wax (slightly lighter than your wood color) into the grain of your table in a circular motion with a rag or the pad on your orbital buffer—truly, a killer use for an orbital buffer. (Tip: You may want to open your windows to deal with the fumes from the scent.) Now go for a walk or rewatch a favorite sitcom episode while you let the wax dry for at least thirty minutes. Then buff the table, again in the direction of the grain, with a soft cotton or microfiber cloth until it shines. (You can buy these waxing items separately or as a kit.)

7. If you don't have a window over your buffet, hang a framed poster, a mirror (perhaps draped with a pom-pom garland), a few plates from Grandma's Blue Willow china, or even mismatched plates collected from yard sales. (So you don't own Flora Danica—the world's most expensive porcelain pattern, first created in 1790 as a gift for Catherine the Great—who cares? A cool plate from a yard sale often flips my pancake.)

Bring a Lot to the Table

And now for the third star in this lineup—the dining room table. With my background in fashion, I like to think of a dining room table as a dress form, or mannequin, you can transform with linens, dinnerware, candles, and more. (That said, a lot of dining room tables are good-looking on their own, without any textiles—a nude table, if you will.)

Most of the time, your dining room table may be empty save for a potted plant, a bowl of apples, or homework and textbooks spread across its expanse. It can also be a great place for kids to hide—or for you to hide stuff—with a floor-length tablecloth. Unless you're actually going to be dining, who's going to know you stash odds and ends under there unless you tell them? And even if you do, they're just going to think you're clever and wish they'd thought of it first.

HL Tip: Wire up Grandma's silver teapot or a great one you found at an estate sale into a charming lamp for your dining room. Or wire several silver items—a teapot, a sugar bowl, and a creamer. Just pick up DIY kits from the hardware store and they'll be ready by teatime.

If you don't want a naked table, here are four ideas:

1. A tablecloth makes, well, of course, the perfect tablecloth—especially if you buy one to your table's exact measurements. But you can get the look of a high-quality tablecloth in a pinch: Just cover your table with a blanket. Next, top the blanket with an ironed sheet. Once the table is set, it'll look fantastic.

2. A remnant from a fabric store can make a great one-of-a-kind tablecloth. And you may not need to even hem it—just iron the edges and tack them down with fabric glue. Easy!

3. Nonconventional tablecloth ideas include a quilt as long as it's not an heirloom (although I could remove any stains), a souvenir throw, and a beach towel, especially for themed dinner events.

4. You can also put multiple linens to work for a unique look: Use a great basic tablecloth and then top it with a multicolored or textured runner across the table to serve as placemats. Or place a long runner lengthwise and then pair it with a couple of short runners across the table for a geometric look. The great thing about runners is they can be as simple as printed cotton or as glitzy as embroidered, beaded velvet with tassels on each end. Like I said—you're dressing your table.

HL Tip: Rather than using and discarding paper napkins, elevate your everyday meals—breakfast, lunch, dinner, snacks, and more—with fabric napkins. And that counts double if they're vintage. Plus, doing so is kinder to the Earth. (If I had children, my dream would be Herkimer and Dorthula fighting over my vintage Christmas napkins.)

I just mentioned the word *placemat*, so I guess I should address the topic. And I have to be honest: I hate placemats. They tend to shift when I set a table, and I'm picky that way. I also associate placemats with the kids' table, not a grown-ups' table. But maybe that's just me.

If you like placemats, there are lots of things you can use besides actual placemats—whimsical dish towels, a favorite fabric cut into rectangles (fray the edges for a cool vibe), even comics for a whimsical Sunday brunch table setting.

Fabric placemats can also be repurposed as cushions for your chairs: Just pair up two matching placemats back-to-back, fill them with poly, and sew or glue them up. (Have a stain on one side? Just flip it over for a clean side.) Or pair one set of placemats with a completely different set of placemats for the opposite side and—voilà!—you've got reversible seat cushions and two completely different looks. Okay, maybe placemats aren't so bad after all.

As a kid, I loved when my mom pulled out all her linens to set the table. I still do today. As they say, she sets a great table. To set off her vintage collection of Noritake Bluedawn, Mom uses two tablecloths: a floor-length blue tablecloth and a smaller white tablecloth. She then pairs her dainty patterned china with her collection of blue crystal glassware and silverware that I sometimes help her polish. When I was young, she actually designed the dining room around her china. That meant there were floor-length blue curtains and a golden tan-striped wallpaper that covered the walls up to the chair rail. It was a formal look for her most formal room.

HL Tip: You can brighten (literally and figuratively) any meal, even frozen pizza, with candles. Just be sure kitchen and dining room candles are unscented or made of beeswax. That way, they won't mess with the aroma and taste of your pepperoni. Salut!

During holidays or after special meals for company, it was Jarrod's and my job to help clear the table. Honestly, I liked carrying all of those special pieces—like the sugar bowl, the gravy boat, and the serving platter—that we only saw once or twice a year. I remember the kitchen being full of the dishes, the glassware, and the silverware—all ready for us to wash and dry. For me, washing dishes is meditative, almost like going to the spa. (Call me crazy, but I know a lot of folks who love washing dishes—and doing laundry, of course.)

My last idea for the dining room table—and it's a good one— focuses on the chairs. If your dining room is expansive and you've got plenty of room to have all the leaves in your table and all the chairs surrounding the table, go for it. But if you're not expecting a party every night, you might consider tucking away those extra leaves, letting your dining room table take up a smaller footprint, and removing a few of those chairs.

Here's the trick: Use a bunch of the dining room chairs around the house—at your kitchen desk, at your desk, even in the bathroom, stacked high with magazines. By doing this, you save money by not having to pay for extra chairs, and when you're hosting a get-together with friends, simply reunite those matching chairs around the dining room table.

One caveat: Who says dining room chairs need to match? Mismatched chairs can add fun and whimsy to your dining room. Or swap out the chair at the head of the table for a wingback, and let the birthday kid (or you) sit on this throne. Or eschew dining room chairs on

HL Tip: While ever-popular votives warm up any table setting, consider using tapers for a romantic touch. If you do add tapers to your candle rotation, be sure to store them flat and wrapped in tissue so they keep their shape.

one side of the table for an upholstered bench or a love seat. Rules, schmools. Do what you want.

Time to Clean Up

Before you ring the dinner bell—tonight or maybe tomorrow night— you've decided to clean your dining space. You'll be glad you took the time to make this room feel welcoming and pleasant for everyone who enjoys it. Keeping in mind the friends and family members (even the furry ones) who share your spaces makes cleaning so much more relax- ing and fun. And might I remind you that cleaning counts as a workout? Especially when you're gearing up for dinner, that's a good thing.

- To begin cleaning your dining room, start at the ceiling, wiping away any cobwebs with a wool duster and brushing off light fix- tures, including cloth shades, with a horsehair brush.
- Next, place everything from your open shelves, top of your side- board or buffet, and the top of your china cabinet onto the dining room table. Doing so enables you to dust all those other surfaces. Begin by dusting the sideboard or buffet with a feather duster or microfiber cloth. I prefer a feather duster, because the feathers grab ahold of the dust so well. But if you've got allergies, stick with the microfiber.
- If you haven't waxed your furniture in six months or more, it's likely time—unless you live somewhere warm; then you only need to wax it once a year. (For how-tos, see "Wax Off, Wax On," page 52.)
- Next, if you've got glass items, now's the time to wash them. Carry them to the kitchen and wash in the sink. However, if these items are just for display, not serving food, feel free to spray a microfiber cloth with the 50/50 vinegar-water solution, and then wipe them down; this treatment should make them sparkle. Clean your china

cabinet's doors the same way and instantly your entire dining room will look so much better.

- If there's a table runner on your sideboard, shake out the dust outside. If it needs a bit more TLC, run a quick load of laundry—including any cloth napkins, table runners, and tablecloths—while you finish cleaning. Before returning these items to your furniture, consider ironing and hitting them with a bit of starch, which will repel stains.

- Once you're done dusting and have returned the items to where they belong, you should have an empty table you can also wax

TWO CLEANS ARE BETTER THAN ONE

Got company coming for dinner? Don't wait until the last minute to clean. You'll feel stressed out and maybe even a bit resentful. Instead, split your cleaning sessions in two: A couple of days before they arrive, do your deep cleaning—mopping the floor, wiping down the walls and windows, dusting and vacuuming, and giving your dining room and kitchen the full treatment. Then, the day of their arrival:

- Do any necessary ten-minute cleans (e.g., the powder room and the bedroom if that's where you'll be placing guests' coats).
- Pick up shared living spaces in your home, returning the odd item to wherever it belongs.
- Wipe down kitchen counters and wash up any dirty dishes (or place them in the dishwasher).
- Plunk a new bouquet of flowers in your entryway.
- Voilà—you're ready!

or dust. The same holds true for your chairs if they're wood. If they're upholstered, check for stains and spot treat with a horsehair brush and a little laundry soap plus warm water. And don't forget to dust the feet of the table, removing any pet hair that's swirled around them.

- If you notice a scratch on your table, touch it up with colored furniture wax or a furniture crayon. Or you can rely on an old-fashioned trick that really works: Crack a fresh walnut and break it in half. Then simply rub the meat of the nut into the scratch. The nut oil will camouflage the scratch for up to a year!

- Lastly, it's time to vacuum up all that dust, the bread crumbs, and more. Be sure to pull the chairs out of the way first.

WHEN WAX ISN'T POETIC

To remove candle wax from a tablecloth or runner, place the item between two layers of kraft paper (or a cut-up grocery bag will work just fine). Then press with a warm iron. The wax will lift right out of the fabric and up into the kraft paper. Then wash the item as normal.

To remove wax drips from a carpet, use the kraft paper trick, and follow up with soap and a brush if needed.

To remove wax from wood furniture, don't scrape or scratch it off. Instead, warm the wax with a hair dryer on low heat. Or you can place a warm, damp cloth inside a ziplock plastic bag and press that down on the wax. When warm enough, the wax can be rolled off, back and forth, with your hand. Then buff the wood with a microfiber cloth.

- Done! Now's a great time to raid your candy stash. What—you don't have one? Then now's the perfect time to start one.

The Ten-Minute Clean: Dining Room

When's a great time for a ten-minute clean of your dining room? When the space needs a spit-and-polish but you don't have enough time for a

---

CREATING A BUTLER'S PANTRY

Where's Jeeves when you need him? I don't know a single person who actually needs a butler, but pretty much everyone needs a butler's pantry. Traditionally, this is a small room, usually located between the kitchen and dining room, mostly used for storing all of the things you need to make entertaining easy and for staging meals while entertaining. Rather than hiding candles under a bathroom sink, displaying platters above your cabinets, and stashing fancy serving spoons in the back of your silverware drawer, a butler's pantry groups all these items together for easy access. If you don't have such a designated room, get creative. It might be that narrow closet in your hallway, an armoire in the corner of your living room, the buffet table in the dining room, or an under-the-bed clear plastic box. What else might you store in there? An extra pitcher, holiday-themed plates, that Champagne bucket you got for your wedding, a centerpiece vase, a deviled egg plate—really anything that makes entertaining easier. You might even tuck a bunch of special cookies or crackers into this hideaway, so you're ready to entertain at a moment's notice.

thorough cleaning. Or when you're going to be entertaining outdoors, but you worry guests might take a gander at your dining room on the way to the loo. Or when you just can't stand the mess anymore. (It's okay. We've all been there.)

- Stash all office equipment or kids' homework or whatever in the buffet, under the table, and/or under the seat cushions. (This tip doesn't work if people will actually dine in the room soon!)
- Make sure all light bulbs are working. If they're dusty, lower the dimmer switch.
- Gather up stray dishes and coffee mugs and place in the dishwasher or kitchen sink.
- Wipe off your table with a microfiber cloth.
- Pull out all the chairs and give the floor a once-over with a broom or vacuum.
- Return the chairs to the table, lining them up nicely.
- If you have a bouquet in a vase, throw out any dead flowers and, if some of the blooms are still fresh looking, refill the vase with new water and return the bouquet to the dining room.
- If you've got an extra forty-five seconds, dump store-bought cookies on a plate and they'll instantly look homemade. Eat one (or two).

HL Tip: Cleaning silverware right before an event feels anticipatory, even meditative, in the best way. Most people rely on silver cleaner to do the job. Other options include polish-impregnated gloves—it's a thing. You simply slip on the gloves and clean the silverware with your hands. In a pinch, ketchup or, more specifically, the acid in the ketchup, makes a gentle silverware cleaner. After polishing, hand-wash and hand-dry it all. Doing this a couple times a year will help keep your silverware in tip-top condition.

My Ten-Minute Cleaning Playlist: Dining Room (Upbeat)

- "It's a Miracle" by Culture Club (3:24)
- "Poison Arrow" by ABC (3:24)
- "Venus" by Bananarama (3:48)

My Ten-Minute Cleaning Playlist: Dining Room (Mellow)

- "A Little More Love" by Olivia Newton-John (3:27)
- "Love for Sale" by Fine Young Cannibals (2:50)
- "Your Love Is King" by Sade (3:39)

HL Tip: Love your china but hardly ever use it? Then make it really shine with a clever washing technique: Hand-wash as normal, but rinse off with a 50/50 ammonia-water solution. Your beloved china will gleam. (However, if you decide to use these dishes for dining, wash again—this time without the ammonia.) You can use this trick with any glass-fronted cabinets as well.

CHAPTER 4

KITCHEN
EVERYTHING PLUS THE KITCHEN SINK

When I cook, it's like a concert on the stove.

—Patti LaBelle

Who says you need a gourmet kitchen? Lots of amazing cooks, famous and otherwise, work in cozy kitchenettes. But if your kitchen is expansive and stunning, I hope you enjoy every inch of it!

And that's the point of refreshing your kitchen—making the entire space work for you.

Certainly, plenty of puny kitchens exist. Think about those in efficiency apartments—known for their mini microwaves, mini fridges, and hot plates—plus those on boats and trains. Even the staff on the Orient Express must create their gourmet meals in two cramped (and moving) kitchens for one hundred passengers multiple times a day.

The smallest kitchen I've ever seen belonged to my friend Louise. The children's book *The Teeny-Tiny Woman* (who lived in a teeny-tiny house) always reminds me of her. Only five-foot-two, this charming woman and my Granny Dude's dear friend created a kitchen so small that only she could stand in it. Perched in front of her stove, Louise could turn ninety degrees to the right to chop onions for her spaghetti sauce, another ninety degrees to place her knife in the sink, and another ninety degrees to reach into the refrigerator for Parmesan cheese.

All of this efficiency was thanks to her own design. A crafty and clever person with mobility challenges, Louise decided to split her childhood home into a duplex so she'd have an easier-to-manage living space plus a slight income. That's when she transformed a former bathroom into her teensy cookery.

But this sweet spot was also aesthetically pleasing. Louise was just that way. Everything—floors, counters, appliances, metal cabinets, and enamel sink—gleamed bright white. But all around the ceiling, shelves showed off her collection of clear bottles of different shapes and sizes, which she had filled with colored water—red, yellow, blue, orange, purple, and green. They lent the room a fun, joyful look.

Getting Inspired

Certainly, Louise's kitchen was the heart of her home. That's true for most of us. And no wonder: It's where you bake your mom's signature cinnamon rolls, whip up your dad's famous pancit, follow Ina's recipe for coconut cupcakes, and slow-cook your best friend's lemony white bean soup. More important, it's where friends and family keep you company, nosh on appetizers, or even help out—chopping veggies, mixing drinks, or decorating cookies.

Even in Louise's Lilliputian kitchen, she kept a stool so I could join her as she cooked. I remember other kitchens belonging to the women of my childhood: In Ibb's immaculate and elegant kitchen, she always had a plate of cheese and crackers ready for my visit; it sat next to a vase of fresh flowers in the summer and a bowl of porcelain fruit in the winter. Ruby's eat-in kitchen had an alcove with a trestle table that made the space feel super cozy. She somehow figured out that I liked filet mignon, and so on countless Thursdays, she'd make me a steak, a baked potato, and a seasonal vegetable—always setting the table with sterling silver.

But it was Granny Dude's kitchen I remember most for countless canning sessions. While Granddad grew a half-acre garden, Granny Dude and my mom would reap the produce rewards, putting up eighty quarts of tomatoes, tomato sauce, tomato juice, and even tomato preserves every summer. I loved the canning hubbub—the boiling pots on the stove, the clink of the jars, and the amazing smells, especially on tomato days. The tomato jars took up every kitchen surface.

And then there was their pickling: pickled beans, pickled beets, pickled cherry tomatoes, pickled corn, and four kinds of cucumber pickles—sweet, dill, ginger, and bread and butter. Plus, they'd put up corn, green beans, and peaches. And I can't forget the apple butter and apple jelly, plum jelly, strawberry jam, grape jelly, and even grape juice. (My mouth is watering!)

Granny and Granddad always made those days an event. At the end of a long canning session, they'd throw burgers on the grill and we'd hang out well into the evening. Meanwhile, the jars would remain in the kitchen overnight to make sure each can "took"—in other words, that no lids popped. Then the jars would be brought down to the cellar.

Growing up, I enjoyed so many meals fresh from the garden in the warmer months and right off the cellar shelves all winter long. I never was a picky eater—how could I be with this abundance?

These days, if you look online, plenty of pantries feature wall-to-wall plastic containers filled with processed foods. They're colorful and pretty. But few things are more compelling to me than rows and rows of Ball jars filled with vibrant, canned produce.

Remembering all of this may sound like yesteryear, but plenty of millennials and even Gen Zers have glommed onto canning, inspired by splashy social media posts, the joy of gardening, healthy living, and caring for the environment. So much so, in fact, that not long ago, there was a shortage of canning jars!

HL Tip: Mason jars are the answer to myriad household needs. Plus, they're charming, whether brand-new and clear or antique and aqua. Use them as great vases, soap dispensers (add pump lids made for that purpose), and luminarias (plunk one tea light in each). Or put them to work in the kitchen—as storage for overnight oats, carry-along salads, and food gifts (e.g., homemade sugar cookies or hot chocolate mix). There are so many more uses! One of my favorites is making whipped cream in sixty seconds. Just add a touch of sugar and ½ teaspoon vanilla extract to 1 cup heavy whipping cream in a Mason jar. Then shake it up. ("I shake it up! I shake it up!" Taylor's song always plays in my head when I do this. Now it will for you too!)

Time to Freshen Up

My goal is to help your kitchen sing—small or large, gourmet or plain Jane. And while remodeling a kitchen can take months of work and cost upward of fifty thousand dollars (or more), refreshing your kitchen can be accomplished in an afternoon and cost anywhere from nothing to a couple hundred dollars. What are you waiting for? Get started with any of these dozen or so ideas, listed in no particular order.

Find more storage, aka time to show off. There's no need to stash away your kitchen supplies and tools. So many kitchen accoutrements are aesthetically pleasing. Plus, if you're short on storage, hanging up your kitchen gear, almost as if it's art, frees up space in your cupboards.

Remember Julia Child, queen of French cooking and public TV for decades? She famously hung up all her copper pans, pots, and utensils

HL Tip: To make delicious ice cream sandwiches, I cut corners: First, I use a boxed mix of brownies, which I bake in a 9 × 13-inch pan lined with foil overhanging the sides. After the brownies have cooled, I use the foil to lift out the brownies. I then cut them horizontally with dental floss; with the floss encircling the rectangle of brownies, I place the end of the floss on the right side in my left hand and the end of the floss on the left side in my right hand and then I pull; the floss slices right through the brownies and separates the top from the bottom in roughly equal halves. I then place the bottom brownie half on a metal serving platter, spread a layer of softened ice cream across it, replace the top brownie layer, and stick it in the freezer to harden. Ten minutes before serving, I remove the pan from the freezer and cut into sandwiches. Simple and tasty!

on a floor-to-ceiling pegboard, even drawing around each item on the board so she knew exactly which tool went where. What a brilliant idea—especially for small spaces short on storage. If that was good enough for Julia, I'm certain it's good enough for us. Bon appétit!

What else do I mean by showing off? How about mounting a ceiling or wall rack to get your pots and pans out of your cupboards and hanging up? Maybe stash your cookie cutters on a mug rack. Rather than fill a drawer with mixing spoons, spatulas, and the like, keep them right at hand by storing them in a basket, antique crock, large vase, or flowerpot (my choice)—on your counter or attached to your wall.

In my kitchen, you'll also find an Arthur Court platter mounted on the wall, a perfect spot considering there's not a single drawer or cupboard in my kitchen that could accommodate it. Besides, I'd rather see this good-looking item every day on my wall than tuck it away on top of my refrigerator where it's out of sight and gathering dust. More important, because it's on display, I use it all the time—not just every Thanksgiving for my turkey and all the trimmings, but also for a simple display of appetizers, to keep my ice cream sandwiches cold (I just throw the platter in the freezer an hour ahead of time), and much more. One thing is for sure: That platter elevates everything I serve.

What pot, pan, or platter might you pull out of your cupboard and hang up? Displaying serving pieces all year round keeps them within reach for entertaining—and for any weeknight dinner. I recommend using L-screws, rather than plate hangers, so platters are securely fastened to the wall but easy to grab. Hang two or three items and suddenly you've got extra cupboard space.

What else can you show off in your kitchen? How about your collection of serving spoons, a trio of colorful colanders, antique ladles, or even foods? Cookies, candies, cereal, and more look great in clear canisters—selected simply for their aesthetics. (*The Golden Girls*' Rose Nylund was right.) Display them on your counter or tuck those canisters away. Every time you open that cupboard, your storage will make you smile!

Lighten up your space. As I noted in a previous chapter, three types of lighting light up any room: ambient (or general) lighting, task lighting, and accent lighting. That's certainly true in the kitchen, where you prep food, eat, and entertain. Making sure your kitchen features all three can be literally illuminating.

To start, look up. Even the most basic kitchen likely has a ceiling light—anything from a dull dome to a spectacular crystal chandelier. My ceiling light fixture is black, industrial, and a bit octopus-y with eight arms, each ending with a bare Edison bulb. Because my ceiling junction box is a bit off-center in my room, I've reconfigured most of the arms to hang directly over my food prep area. (You'd likely never notice unless I pointed it out.) This light fixture checks the ambient

HL Tip: Love lemons? Here are three great ways to put five lovely lemons to work in your kitchen:

First, cut one lemon in half and dip both exposed sides in salt. Then go to town on your countertops (don't do this if you have marble or quartz countertops); lemon's citric acid will scrub away all drips and drops, even from stainless steel! Plus, it's a natural disinfectant! Then just wipe off the counter with a damp cloth to remove any traces of lemon juice and salt.

Second, to clean your garbage disposal, cut the second lemon into four pieces, then drop them down the sink and run your disposal. Not only will the lemon's citric acid clean your disposal, but your sink will now smell great too!

Finally, with the three remaining lemons, make lemonade. (Doesn't a tall, cold glass sound great after all that cleaning?) Quarter the lemons and squeeze the juice into a measuring cup. Whatever the total, likely a ½ cup, add the matching amount of sugar, in this case another ½ cup, to the measuring cup. The lemon juice will dissolve the sugar. Then pour the solution into a pitcher, add 3 cups cold water, stir, and drink. Ah!

and task lighting boxes and, while it's ten years old, it still makes me happy.

Do you love or hate your ceiling light? Or maybe you've never given it a whole lot of thought. Maybe it's a bit milquetoast, glowing softly but offering no personality. A truly great light should both fulfill its function and serve as décor. If yours is lackluster, you can upgrade a light, even in a rental. Consider adding an oversized shade to dress it up, or, if it's got a bunch of individual lights like mine, clip-on shades. You can also replace that 60-watt incandescent bulb with a 15-watt LED for twice the light and a fraction of the energy.

HL Tip: This tip is so good that it should be included on every page of the book or in a very large font. If you're going to dog-ear a page in *House Love*, let it be this one.

"Oh, I can't take credit—it's Donna Ekberg's recipe." That's often my response when someone asks about a dish I've prepared. It's an inside joke, but now I'll let you in on it: Years ago I asked Donna—a customer, consummate hostess, and dear friend—what she serves her family for Christmas. When she told me lasagna, I asked for her recipe. "Oh, it's so easy," she said with a twinkle in her eye. "First, I buy a giant frozen lasagna. Then I cut it into pieces to fit into my Le Creuset baking pan. I pour tomato sauce over the top, dump mozzarella cheese on top, and bake."

I so loved her devil-may-care response that ever since I've often followed her lead. For example, want my recipe for baked beans? Just mix together two or three flavors of canned baked beans—say, bourbon, brown sugar, and Southern barbecue—in your Dutch oven and heat. Absolutely delicious! And when someone asks for the recipe, just say, "Oh, I can't take credit—it's Donna Ekberg's recipe."

So next time you're rushed or just don't feel like cooking, remember, you can make Donna's recipe tonight. You're welcome.

To replace the light completely, purchase a new fixture you love and a conversion kit from a hardware store. If your house was built before 1985, I'd recommend hiring an electrician to ensure your wiring is up to code and your new light fixture will work safely. If your house is newer and you're handy, watch a YouTube how-to video and be sure to turn off the electricity to that room before attempting. If you're not handy, hire an electrician for this quick job.

Next up is task lighting, especially important if you're making coffee, slicing carrots, or pouring yourself a glass of Chardonnay. Like I mentioned, my ceiling light partly covers my task lighting needs. But I also have under-cabinet task lighting for close-up work.

What's your task lighting sitch? Perhaps pendants hang over your kitchen island, but a second prep space is located far from those lights. Or maybe you like your ceiling light fixture but have no real task lights. Then it's time to throw some light, so to speak, on the situation. Myriad under-cabinet lights exist these days—from high-tech, direct-wired modular tracks with puck lights to do-it-yourself, stick-on, battery-operated options. Of course, the price for task lighting covers a broad range as well. Your choice will depend on what you're looking for, whether your home is rented, and what your budget can cover. I'd recommend doing a bit of research before making your selection.

Even easier? Plug in a small lamp on your counter—this super homey touch is an unexpected option. Lastly, you can even use task lighting inside your cabinets and your drawers to make distinguishing your cardamom from your cinnamon and your peeler from your pepper mill all the easier.

HL Tip: I keep multiple measuring spoon sets on hand. That way, when I'm cooking, I don't have to keep constantly washing a single set. Call me lazy—or a genius!

Last up is accent lighting. In my first apartment, I placed a string of old-fashioned Christmas lights (the big ones) on top of my cabinets and added a timer so they'd automatically turn on every evening. It was a welcome sight when I'd come home late at night.

Today, there are so many more options. Plug in a Himalayan salt light, turn on battery-operated candles, or drape a lighted garland across the top of your cabinets. Or add battery-operated fairy lights practically anywhere—you only need to replace the batteries a couple times a year. You can tuck them in at the toe-kick with a staple gun. Or throw them in a frosted pitcher to serve as a lovely night-light.

Speaking of nightlights, literally hundreds of options can light your way to a midnight snack. A friend of mine bought a dozen matching automatic nightlights and uses them throughout her house on any outlet that doesn't sport a plug; they serve almost like aisle lights in a movie theater.

In addition to a nightlight in my kitchen, plus the chandelier and under-cabinet lighting, visitors always notice my carrot sconces and carrot marquee light. What accent lights make sense for your kitchen? What light might make your kitchen all the more welcoming and a place you and your visitors want to spend time?

Throw in the towels. For a small investment that packs a fun punch, buy a bunch of vibrant dish towels that reflect you and your interests. Dish towels used to be boring and utilitarian, but no more.

HL Tip: To clean a copper pot or pan, reach into your refrigerator and grab your bottle of ketchup. Yes, that's right—you're going to put the naturally occurring acid in that classic condiment to work. Add a squirt of ketchup to a paper towel and use it like a cleaner, smearing it around to bring back the gleam to that copper. Amazing, right? Rinse, dry, and you're done with that ketchup until your next hankering for fries.

Whether you love candy or carrots, rocks or rock music, dachshunds or Depression glass, you can find a dish towel for that—at online marketplaces, cute boutiques, far-flung cities where you vacation, or even mega discount stores.

Plus, kitchen towels are a fun and inexpensive way to signal a new season. You might prefer gingham or striped towels, plain or whimsical towels, or old-fashioned flour sack towels embroidered by your granny or neighbor whose rummage sale you hit up.

Whatever you choose, rather than keep them tucked away in a drawer, stash them in a basket—on your counter or on a wall—where you can see and enjoy them every day.

TWO DISHCLOTH GIFT-GIVING IDEAS

First, it's likely your grandma or great-grandma had a few calendar dishcloths, miniature yearlong calendars featured on dish towels and hung as kitchen décor all year long. When a new year would roll around, the old calendar dishcloth would transition to its practical use and a new one would be posted. If you know someone who loves to cook or loves vintage, consider giving them a dish towel from the year of their birth. You can even find new colorful dishcloths for the current year online.

Second, a dish towel makes great gift-wrap, especially if your present is kitchen-related, say a jar of jam and a decorative jam spoon. Just place the items in the center of the dish towel's backside, fold up the four corners, and tie. Easy! A friend of mine did this on Valentine's Day, filling a variety of red-and-white dish towels with pinwheel mint candies, and giving them to friends and family.

Dish towels are also practical, lessening the need for paper towels and napkins. Use them not just to dry your dishes, but also as counter cleaners, hand wipers, and napkins. When you're entertaining, place a favorite dish towel in a basket to hold croissants or under a platter to show off your charcuterie assortment. I've even seen dish towels designed to loop around a paper towel holder—they can be used, washed, and used again and again.

Decorate your kitchen with carrots. Not really—that's my thing. I have carrot platters, a carrot tablecloth, carrot cookie cutters, and more. (Yes, I really do.) But your thing might be birds, quilts, or motorcycles. Why not personalize your kitchen with the things you love? Doing so will make you happy.

Throw it at the kitchen wall and see what sticks—just like a perfectly cooked strand of spaghetti. Here's a bunch more kitchen refresh ideas to consider:

- **Make a splash with your backsplash.** Don't have a backsplash? For a (very) small price, create a backsplash with removable wallpaper. These days, you can find it everywhere in all kinds of colors, patterns, and textures. Removable wallpaper is easy to wipe down and, of course, easy to remove—especially important if you live in a rental. You might even consider covering a wall or your whole kitchen in removable wallpaper. Perhaps you've always wanted to live in a loft with an exposed brick wall. Now you can—with exposed brick wallpaper. One more idea: If you have a tile backsplash that you can't stand, you can actually paint over it with an epoxy refinishing tile kit and any color paint you wish. Just be sure to follow the directions and prep the backsplash well.

- **Paint the kitchen red.** Or blue or your favorite color. Painting isn't hard and a gallon or less should cover all the walls of nearly any kitchen. Decide in a year, or a month, that you don't love it? Choose a new color and repaint. Plus, even if you're in a rental, you might get permission to paint your kitchen—or perhaps a single wall. In my first apartment, my landlord gave me the go-ahead to paint as long as I used a color that met his approval. He okayed my selection of green—let's call it Granny Smith apple.

- **Be completely floored.** A thick rug or two will offer cushioning for your feet while you cook and provide a nice contrast with the hard surfaces of a kitchen. And because rugs in the kitchen are sure to experience drips and splashes, be sure they're washable. In my neutral space, I've got a doormat and a larger rug, both purchased at an art fair and both in a lively orange. Mine are rag rugs. If you too like rag rugs, here's a fun idea: Select a bunch of con-

SQUIRREL AWAY

Squirrels are among my least favorite animals, but I do love their practice of squirreling away food. That's the whole idea behind a pantry. My mom has a pantry to this day, and she fills oodles of glass jars of all different sizes and colors with beans, cereal, coffee, popcorn kernels, rice, and every other foodstuff you can imagine.

When I was growing up, Granny Dude did the same. One of my fondest memories is stepping into her pantry, the sun shining through the casement windows and lighting up the hundreds of jars of foods of every color stacked floor to ceiling. There's the beauty of the jars and then there's the practicality: Glass jars last forever—some of my mom's jars are nearly eighty years old. Plus, they keep out all insects. You can buy in bulk, which minimizes the waste of buying multiple containers.

HL Tip: Always keep a scrub brush handy. Then, while waiting for something to boil or while chatting with your bestie on the phone, grab it for a quick project, like scrubbing around your faucet or brushing crumbs from under your toaster.

trasting or complementary rag rugs and loosely stitch their edges together to cover a larger section of floor. If you decide you want to use them separately later on, just snip the stitches. Be sure also to use rug tape or include a nonslip mat underneath any rugs you add to your kitchen.

- **Convert your cabinet pulls.** In my first apartment, I splurged on six carrot knobs at five dollars a pop for my upper cabinets. These days, my cabinet knobs are a bit more reserved. Could new knobs transform your space? You bet. Find dozens of options at your local hardware store, online, and at flea markets. Consider colorful glass knobs, mismatched antique knobs, and wooden knobs that you can paint. One friend used mismatched old silverware, bending the handles to serve as cabinet pulls—she even used a pie server and ladle on her refrigerator door.

- **Switch up your switch plates.** My backsplash is mirrored and so I selected mirrored light switch plates to blend right in. Or maybe you want to find switch plates that match your walls or your light fixtures. Or cover your switch plates with that removable wallpaper you used for your backsplash. Regardless, it's these small details—nightlights, cabinet knobs, switch plates, and the like—that can add up to create a new look. Especially in a small space, every detail matters.

- **Bring a garden inside.** Grow a favorite herb or two on your kitchen windowsill or countertop. I'd suggest planting your favorites, but if you're looking for guidance, consider thyme (my num-

HL Tip: There are lots of great ideas for kitchen organization. If you're a coffee or tea drinker, here's a good one: Treat yourself to your own coffee/tea station by keeping everything within easy reach. That includes your coffee and tea, of course, plus your coffee maker, burr grinder, electric teakettle, teapot, mugs, and teacups. But don't stop there: Pour on the caffeine with coffee- or tea-themed kitchen towels, long-handled mixing spoons, white and brown sugar cubes, maple and flavored syrups, honey, chocolate chips, ground cardamom, and nutmeg. And don't forget a cookie jar! You could even add a cute counter fridge for cold coffee and tea, creamers, and half-and-half. I'm not even a major coffee drinker and I want to do this right now!

ber one choice), basil, and chives—three flavorful additions to lots of dishes. (Also, you can add a couple of sprigs of thyme to your 50/50 vinegar-water solution, and your spray's antibacterial properties are boosted, thanks to the thymol in thyme.) Grow basil in the summer for your margaritas and guacamole, and chives in the winter because you're obsessed with baked potatoes. Growing herbs not only adds greenery and an amazing smell to your kitchen, but it will also save you lots of money since you won't be buying herbs every time you attempt that *New York Times* Cooking recipe you've been wanting to try.

- **Master the art of the kitchen.** While kitchens tend to be utilitarian, why not hang a favorite artwork in the space—whether it's your kid's latest masterpiece, a rummage sale find, or a wooden platter you inherited from Aunt Marvel. You also might consider adding a trio of decorative tiles over your kitchen window, dressing up your backsplash with a couple of small art prints, or hanging a vintage chalkboard. Or buy a rummage sale painting and repaint the center with chalkboard paint. (You could also just paint a wall or your kitchen door with chalkboard paint.) Then personalize that chalkboard daily or weekly with notes to loved ones, welcome messages to guests, grocery lists, or favorite sayings. In my kitchen, as in many, the breaker box is located on one wall. My artsy solution? I hung a decorative quilted wall hanging right over it.

- **Make yours a trash can to treasure.** Many of us use a simple plastic garbage can that hides under the kitchen sink. Instead, consider gaining back that bit of storage and adding a personality-plus garbage can that lives large in your kitchen. I've had my tall, orange garbage can for nearly twenty years. Yes, I paid a premium for it, but it's well made and has added a jolt of happy to my space ever since. But maybe you don't need a giant garbage can. You can find inexpensive, hardworking galvanized cans at the hardware store in myriad sizes. Choose the size that best fits your space. A small one also works great for composting, especially if it has a tight-fitting lid. Oh, and one more thing: If you don't love the

HL Tip: I've got a freestanding convection burner. Much like a hot plate, it cost me less than a hundred dollars and gives me the freedom to cook just about anywhere. I've even brought it to my store where a caterer once whipped up, not pigs in blankets, but tiny portions of coq au vin and quail egg apps. Most of the time, though, I just use it on my kitchen peninsula, chopping up veggies for soup and letting that medley simmer while I make something else on my stove. You can even use a convection burner outside—especially if you're cooking something pungent, say asparagus, bacon, or fish, or if it's just too hot to heat up the kitchen. Who needs a fancy outdoor kitchen when you've got a convection burner?

galvanized look, you can prime and spray-paint a can any color
you wish.

- **You can't live on bread alone.** New and vintage canisters labeled
Flour, Sugar, and the like can add a lot of personality to your
kitchen and are great for storing all kinds of things. If you don't
bake, maybe you store cereal in your flour canister, dog treats in
your sugar canister, and coffee in your tea canister. Or maybe you
store medicines and vitamins, your first aid kit, or all those take-
out sauces that pile up. A friend of mine uses her vintage metal
bread box for kitchen compost; another uses hers for laundry supplies. (I approve.)

- **Maximize your space.** My kitchen isn't large, so I make every
square inch count. Case in point: To gain more counter space, I
replaced a standard wood windowsill with one made of granite.
Now I've got an extra surface to place anything coming hot out of
the oven. Plus, in warmer months, my neighbors get to enjoy my
baking—or at least the scent of my raspberry pies cooling. Where
might you gain more space? Think outside the box and you'll
undoubtedly find extra space.

Time to Clean Up

Cleaning the kitchen feels like a nearly never-ending task. Three meals
a day plus some snacks add up to dirty dishes, drips on the countertop,
and spills on the floor. You've got all that handled—for the most part.
But once a week, it's a good idea to do the real deal—the not-a-crumb-
on-the-counter, not-a-drip-on-the-floor clean. I find that inviting people over is my best motivation to do this all-encompassing scrub. But
you might have something else motivating you—the plumber's house
call tomorrow, a family birthday, a seasonal equinox. Whatever works!
Wearing my cleaning outfit, including my Culture Club T-shirt, helps.
As does a giant Diet Coke and the right tunes. Before I know it, the

kitchen is gleaming and I have to pull on my shades. Get yours ready, because here we go.

- To clean your kitchen, start at the ceiling, wiping away any cobwebs with a wool duster. Next, turn off your lights and brush off fixtures, including cloth shades, with a horsehair brush. If your lights are not only dusty but also sticky, spray a towel with a 50/50 vinegar-water solution, and then wipe down. Or you might want to dedicate a pair of pet-drying towel mitts to your pendant lights for easy cleaning. Finally, make sure all your light bulbs are working; if one or more are on the blink, replace as needed.
- Empty the dishwasher of its clean dishes and/or fill it up with their dirty equivalents.

HL Tip: From cakes to casseroles, apple pies to pizza pies, and so much more, cast iron makes a great choice, thanks to its ability to heat up slow and steady and retain heat. Plus, cast iron is built to endure, so you could be cooking with your grandma's pans—or someday your grandkids might be cooking with yours!

To make cast iron last, simply rub your skillet with coarse kosher salt, removing any cooking food particles with a pan scraper; then apply a thin layer of an unsaturated fat like canola, olive, or vegetable oil (not saturated fats like coconut or palm oil) and store until its next use.

If your pan is rusted (or you scored a rusted cast-iron one at an estate sale), sprinkle it with baking soda, a drop of dish soap, and water, and then get scrubbing. Now rinse and dry the skillet; then flip it over and repeat those steps. Next, rub a layer of shortening into both sides of the pan, and bake it upside down on a sheet pan for an hour at 350°F. Now turn off the oven and remove the pan when it's completely cool.

- Spray a clean terrycloth towel with the vinegar solution and wipe down the exterior of your cabinets; be sure to clean the cabinet knobs as well.

- Spray the stove and countertops with the vinegar solution and wipe down. But if you've got granite or stone countertops, spray instead with vodka—vinegar is too acidic.

- If there's baked-on enchiladas or who-knows-what on any of your surfaces, feel free to spray them again and then scrub with a soft horsehair brush.

- If your sink is relatively clean, wipe down with the vinegar solution. If it needs a little more oomph, clean with baking soda or Bar Keepers Friend powder cleaner. Then, once or twice a year, pull out your orbital buffer to gently do away with any fine layer of buildup. When you do, you'll be amazed at how glossy your porcelain sink or shiny your metal sink becomes.

- Spray the exterior of the refrigerator with the vinegar solution and wipe down the entire surface, paying particular attention to the handles and the area around them. Next, turn to the interior: Discard or compost old fruits and vegetables, and throw out any meat items past their prime. If you've got the time, remove everything from one shelf at a time, spraying the shelf with the vinegar

HL Tip: Is it challenging to differentiate the aluminum foil from the wax paper from the plastic wrap in all of those long matching boxes tucked away in a cupboard? Simply remove the rolls from the boxes and store them vertically in a large vase or bucket under the sink. True, you won't have each box's serrated edge for cutting, but you may find ripping works just as well. (Oh, and recycle those boxes; just pull off and discard the serrated edges first.)

BEFORE HELL FREEZES OVER

Cleaning your freezer needs to happen only once a year, and it's not as hard as you think (as opposed to those meatballs you threw into the freezer two years ago).

- First, toss any food you can't identify or is left over from the Clinton administration. (Hot Pockets, Bagel Bites, and mini quiches—or is that the Nixon era?)
- Next, place the food you're saving into coolers with plenty of ice and/or ice packs.
- Now unplug your freezer.
- Place an old towel topped by a cookie sheet underneath the freezer door to soak up drips.
- Take out any removable shelves and drawers, and let them warm up before washing them with hot, soapy water. Let them air-dry, or dry them with a dish towel.
- If your freezer is a newer, self-defrosting model, there should be no need to defrost or remove ice from the walls. Instead, grab a spray bottle filled with half vinegar and half hot water, and spray the freezer's walls, floor, and rubber parts, wiping them dry as you go with a sponge or microfiber cloth.
- If it's an older freezer that requires defrosting, fill a pan with hot water and place it on the freezer's floor for a few minutes. Then gently remove the melting ice with a plastic spatula—not with any tool that's sharp, which can cause damage.
- Once the freezer is defrosted, return to the vinegar-and-hot-water method, cleaning both the inside and

the outside of the freezer, and dry both. Finally, dust the
condenser coils on the back.
- Now return all the shelving and food to your freezer,
  plug it back in, and go take a nap.

solution, wiping it down, and then returning the items to it. Once
every month or so, it's a good idea to actually remove the shelves
and wash them with hot soapy water in the sink. Repeat these
steps for the freezer, and finally, wipe down the floor of the refrigerator and freezer. Don't forget to dust off the coils under the
refrigerator or behind it—they can get dusty even if your home
is immaculate. Once every other month, pull out the refrigerator
and discover treasures: a toy from a fast-food kid's meal, a battery,
dry dog food, and that earring you thought was lost forever.

- Spray the exterior of the microwave with the vinegar solution and
  wipe it down. Next, spray the microwave interior with the vinegar
  solution and add a cup of vinegar to a glass measuring cup. Place the
  cup inside the microwave and turn it on for two minutes at 50 percent
  power. This should help loosen any gunk in the microwave, making
  wiping away all grease and food bits easy. Finally, remove the glass
  platter, wash it in the sink, dry it, and return it to the microwave.

- Unplug any small appliances, spray a clean cloth with the vinegar
  solution, and wipe down their exteriors. For a toaster in particular, unplug and use a small brush to gently remove crumbs from
  the slots. Then remove the bottom tray and dump the crumbs
  into the sink, organics container, or garbage. Next, wash the tray,
  rinse, and dry before returning it to the toaster. Finally, gently tip
  the toaster upside down over the sink or garbage and shake out
  any remaining crumbs.

FLOWER POWER AND A WHOLE LOT MORE

Summer is the most flowery of seasons. Show-off. Is there ever a reason not to have flowers on display in the summer? While fresh blooms look great in every room in the house, a bouquet in the kitchen where you and your guests can enjoy it is always a good idea. Grab a bunch of flowers at a florist, grocery store, or farmer's market. Cut them from your garden. Or even pick a bunch of dandelions—then tie them with a ribbon and plunk your posy into a jam jar. Now that's a jolt of joy. Again, summertime flowers are easy. But what about the rest of the year? What follows are ideas for your kitchen and throughout your home. (Did you know I used to be a floral designer?)

In the fall

- Tuck into a tall floor vase a few branches of leaves from a tree in your yard or your local florist. Then place a lamp nearby to cast a cool silhouette on your wall—so chic and easy, and it costs next to nothing.
- Let sunshine pour through a collage of colored leaves in a window. Place found leaves between two sheets of wax paper, usually coated with paraffin, lay a kitchen towel over the sheets, and then press with a warm (not hot) iron until the sheets adhere to each other. Easy!
- Gather or purchase an odd number of decorative gourds and pair them with vintage books or a small mirror for a lovely autumnal display on your fireplace mantel.

- Scatter colored leaves across your dining room table; while kids wait to eat, they can do leaf rubbings, placing leaves beneath sheets of paper and then coloring on the paper with crayons or colored pencils. (Honestly, this is fun for people of any age.)

In the winter

- Winter brings to mind pine branches and cones, poinsettias, holly berries, and white birch branches—all are good choices that can put you in the mood for the holidays.
- Or use objects you love as a centerpiece, say a wooden bowl filled with nuts and an interesting nutcracker, a small collection of stones or shells, or a tall cylindrical clear vase filled with green apples.
- Enjoy spring in the midst of winter with amaryllis, crocuses, daffodils, hyacinths, paperwhites, or tulips. Doing so involves forcing, or what might better be called faking. You're faking spring conditions so that the bulbs will bloom early. Simply plant the bulbs, root side down, in well-drained potting mix; water; and then set the pot in a cool, dark spot (not in a below-freezing garage) for two to four months, depending on the type of bulb. (Find directions online or on the package.) During this time, be sure to water anytime the soil on top is dry to the touch. Once the bulbs have grown roots, you can bring the pot inside, where the warmth and sunshine will prompt the bulbs to grow. In the midst of winter's dark days, spring flowers are such a pick-me-up and lovely in any room of your house.

- If you live where spring tends to arrive late, consider introducing some old-fashioned and cheerful flowers to your house: African violets or primroses. Violets are easy to grow year-round indoors and come in a bevy of colors: white, pink, lavender, deep purple, and variegated. Primroses only bloom for a few weeks indoors; after the flowers fade, many people simply discard the plant or they may plant it outdoors in the summer and then bring it back inside in the fall, allowing for a month or two of dormancy.

In the spring

- To prep for summer gardening and save money, start your flowers from seeds and then plant them outside when summer arrives. Flowers that do well from seed include alyssum, celosia, cosmos, morning glories, petunias, phlox, and zinnias. I particularly love blue petunias, which are super challenging to find as plants at nurseries, so it's not uncommon for me to grow my own from seeds.
- If you've got flowers to share, say a plethora of lilacs, cut a few bunches and bring them to your neighbors. Or do as a friend's neighbor did and post a sign inviting passersby to pick a few flowers from her burgeoning alleyway garden. What a delight!
- If you celebrate Easter, cut a two- to three-foot bare branch with lots of offshoot branches and then spray-paint it white, pink, or even silver. Place the branch into a pot filled with plaster of Paris, wait for it to dry, and then hang Easter eggs from the spindly branches.

- And don't forget about the ubiquitous spring blooms: daffodils, forsythia, peonies, pussy willows, tulips, and flowering trees, like cherry blossoms. Any of these growing outside or gathered together in bursting bouquets or small arrangements can introduce spring to your home.

- During the summer, when you can open the windows, use the self-cleaning feature of your oven. During the rest of the year, I'd recommend spraying the interior with water, sprinkling with baking soda, and then spraying again, this time with vinegar. Next, while the vinegar and baking soda do their jobs, foaming up, go take Romo for a walk, water your houseplants, or read the next chapter (or two) in a book. Return when you're done and you should find it a cinch to wipe away the foam and the gunk.
- Spray a microfiber cloth or newspaper with the vinegar solution and wipe down any windows and glass-fronted art.

HL Tip: On a rainy day, spend a fun afternoon making tissue flowers with your friends or kids. These ephemeral, creative posies go back hundreds of years. Dozens of tutorials can be found online and in craft magazines and books. Then use your creations for all kinds of home projects, including floral wreaths and banners, dressing up a party table, and decorating a bedroom door or bulletin board.

- Roll up kitchen rugs to keep the crumbs inside and shake them out in your garbage can or outdoors. Before bringing them back in, vacuum or sweep the floor. If the floor could use more than a quick sweep, spray the areas that need extra cleaning with the vinegar solution and wipe dry. Or, if you've got a steam cleaner, use that multitasker to disinfect, sanitize, degrease, deodorize, and clean your floor.
- Discard any dead flowers or sad-looking produce on display into your compost or garbage.
- Carry out the garbage, recycling, and compost, and replace the bag in each bin.
- Throw into the wash any used kitchen towels and replace with freshly laundered ones.
- Lastly, admire your gleaming kitchen and treat yourself to something a bit extra—microwave popcorn, a cup of coffee with cream ("Would you like coffee with that cream?"), or a cookie warmed up in your freshly cleaned microwave—you deserve it!

The Ten-Minute Clean: Kitchen

Some people don't entertain because they never feel like their house is ready—even after a major cleaning session. We need to let down our guards and our unachievable standards. You've got some clean dishes, a

HL Tip: With faded roses, you can make an easy potpourri. Once the flowers have lost their bloom, spread the rose petals on a cookie sheet and tuck it into a chilly closet. After a few days, distribute the dried petals—along with cinnamon sticks, star anise, and dried lavender (from your local farmer's market or co-op)—among tulle jewelry bags to create sachets for yourself and loved ones.

few cloth napkins, maybe a bottle of wine or some lemonade? Go ahead and invite the neighbors over. Order a pizza or throw some cheeses and grapes on a plate. Good enough, I say. People are coming over to see you, not your house. But if it's a last-minute occasion and you feel the need to clean, let this speedy kitchen-cleaning approach be your guide.

- Make sure all light bulbs are working—if they're not, turn off the lights and light a couple of candles.
- Gather stray dishes and coffee mugs, and place them in the dishwasher. (If the dishwasher is full of clean dishes, just stack the dirty ones in the sink.)
- Spray a cloth with the 50/50 vinegar-water solution and then wipe down the cabinet knobs and touch up the cabinets.
- Give the sink, faucet, and countertops a wipe down with a damp washcloth and the vinegar solution.
- Wipe down the front of the microwave and stove.
- Wipe down the refrigerator handle and touch up the refrigerator floor.
- Shake out any kitchen rugs into the garbage and sweep or vacuum the floor.
- Throw out any dead flowers or sad-looking produce into your composting bin or garbage.
- Lastly, grab a spoon and your ice cream, and eat a few bites straight from the carton. Or plunk down on your couch and dive into that article that you've been meaning to read. You deserve some "me" time.

My Ten-Minute Cleaning Playlist: Kitchen (Upbeat)
- "Stir It Up" by Patti LaBelle (3:38)
- "Levitating" by Dua Lipa (3:23)
- "Ask" by the Smiths (3:16)

My Ten-Minute Cleaning Playlist: Kitchen (Mellow)

- "A Case of You" by Jane Monheit (4:28)
- "Town Without Pity" by Gene Pitney (2:54)
- "And She Was" by Talking Heads (3:37)

HL Tip: You've enjoyed the world's best lasagna, but now you have to clean that baked-on mess. No problem: Simply stopper up your sink and fill it with warm water. Now mix in 1 or 2 table-spoons sodium percarbonate and set the pan in the water to soak for a half hour. No matter what type of pots and pans you use, the oxygen bleach will lift the pasta remnants right off.

CHAPTER 5

BEDROOM
CALLING IT A GOOD NIGHT

*Think what a better world it would be if we all, the whole
world, had cookies and milk about three o'clock every
afternoon and then lay down on our blankets for a nap.*

—Robert Fulghum

Tidy. Now there's a word that perhaps rarely pops to mind when thinking of our bedrooms. Yet many of us dream of staying in a luxurious hotel room, imagining it to be both the pinnacle of living and sleeping. I'd suggest that it's not the room's splendor, view, or bed that makes it so dreamy, but its cleanliness and, honestly, its lack of stuff. There's no unmade bed, no messy closet, no clothes on the floor, no stacks of books, no old coffee cups, no earplugs, no lotions, and no laundry basket.

Instead, as you step into that deluxe hotel room, there's often a gasp of appreciation as your eyes rest on the welcoming display: the bed, its crisp linens pulled taut, and its pillows, plumped and perfect. There are the bedside tables (displaying only lovely lamps), the sophisticated wall coverings, the compelling art, and the multicolored patterned carpet.

How often does your bedroom look like this? Always? Sometimes? Never? We spend roughly a third of our lives sleeping plus more time in this room dressing, reading, watching TV, and (ahem) doing other things. All of these activities are great reasons not only to refresh your bedroom but also to keep it tidy, ensuring it's a restful place where you want to spend time. As novelist Stella Gibbons once wrote, "Unless everything is tidy and pleasant and comfortable . . . people cannot even begin to enjoy life."

My family visited lots of historic homes on our vacations, and every time I spotted one of those grand four-poster canopy beds, I was

HL Tip: So you love the idea of tranquil bedroom walls. That doesn't mean you can't hide a splash of daring inside your closet. Just spin that paint wheel to find an option that complements your wall color. I guarantee you'll smile every time you open the closet door.

mesmerized. As a child, I could only imagine what it might feel like to close up those curtains and crawl under piles of featherbeds—perhaps, I thought, a bit like sleeping in a pillow fort but better. Way better. Years later, in my first apartment, my dream kind of came true when I slept in an alcove that accommodated both my bed and my reading lamp—so cozy.

Whether sleeping in a canopy, an alcove, or even a tent, most of us love that feeling of privacy in our bedrooms. Interestingly, the word *bedchamber*, derived from both French and Middle English, means a space for sleeping. Yet a private room dedicated to sleeping was a relatively new concept adopted by Victorians at all levels of society. Previously, even large families slept together in a single bed or room, and colonial inns offered communal bedrooms for traveling strangers. (I'd rather sleep in the barn with the cows and the sheep, thank you very much.)

Consider one-room cabins: The living space was used for cooking, baking, washing, drying, mending, bathing, sleeping, and more. Today, while the activities may have changed a bit, a studio apartment is still employed in the same way. Plus, even if you live in a single-family home, you might use your bedroom for a whole array of activities, including working—perhaps setting up a corner desk to serve both as home office and home studio for all those virtual meetings. So there's another reason you might want to refresh your bedroom—if you're spending your waking and sleeping hours in it, you deserve to make it a sanctuary.

HL Tip: A bedroom is a great place to display personal items, even heirlooms—whether that's your grandma's kimono, your mom's favorite scarf, your dad's baby shoes, your spelling-bee trophy, or your childhood quilt. Consider framing this special item or displaying it in a place of honor.

HL Tip: Feature a boudoir photo or two in your bedroom. No, not necessarily that kind of boudoir photo. The term *boudoir* simply means *bedroom*. Maybe it's a picture of you and your best friend hamming it up—a photo that makes you laugh but one you don't necessarily share with everyone who visits your home. Consider printing and framing your favorites—then display them together.

HL Tip: Don't feel you need to stick to standard bedroom furniture. For example, as I mentioned before, my former kitchen table serves as one of my nightstands. Other ideas might include using a military trunk as a bench at the foot of your bed, a stack of vintage suitcases as a side table, or a bar cart as a makeup vanity.

I used to know a guy who had an unusual bedroom. Because he worked in fashion, he needed to look his best and owned an abundance of clothes. Unfortunately, his apartment was small. His clever solution? He dedicated the front half of his living room to a seating area and the back half to his bedroom, dividing the spaces with his couch. Meanwhile, what had been the bedroom became a giant walk-in closet. It made all the sense in the world for his life and his career. To top it off, he infused his sense of style into all of these spaces, layering them with opulent and creative furnishings. In a phrase, he made his bedroom, and his home, his own. That's exactly what I wish for you.

Time to Freshen Up

Before we dive into a dozen ways to revitalize your bedroom, I'll offer one more metaphor: Many brides spend five hundred dollars or more on a pair of shoes they'll wear for less than a day, yet they spend a hundred dollars or less on a pair of shoes they wear every day. The same goes for that luxury hotel room and your bedroom at home. Doesn't it make sense to invest more in the room you sleep in nearly every night? Enough said. Time to refresh.

Change your sheets. There's nothing more essential to your bedroom than bedding. And that hotel bed isn't more comfortable because it's got white sheets. It's because they're fresh, clean, and crisp. Any color sheets will do. What matters is their feel. The lower the thread count, the crisper the sheets. The higher the thread count, the silkier the sheets. To determine your preference—for example, cotton, bamboo, linen, or perhaps a 50/50 cotton/poly combo (like many hotels use)—you need to feel them. These days you can even find really great sheets at discount stores. And don't be afraid to return or

HL Tip: Thinking about donating that old baby blanket with the holes in it or that pieced quilt that's seen better days? Now, hold up there a moment. Quite literally, you can save that special item and get something new to boot. Vintage blankets and quilts can be remade as headboards, tablecloths, sofa throws, cushion covers, throw pillows, Christmas-tree skirts, and more. If you're clever with a sewing machine or a needle and thread, more power to you. If you're all thumbs when it comes to sewing or you just don't have the time, consider tapping a tailor for help. And then you never have to say good-bye to that special something.

CLEANING BAXTER'S BED

Just like your bed linens, your furry friend's bed needs cleaning, preferably once or even twice a month. Here's how:

- **For a Poly-fil bed:** Simply throw it into a front- or top-
loading washing machine and wash as normal with 1
tablespoon of laundry soap and 1 tablespoon of oxygen bleach; the latter will remove any oil from your
pet's coat. Then lay the bed over a rack to dry; when
completely dry, throw it in the dryer on the no-heat, air-
fluff setting with a couple of clean tennis balls for serious fluffing. If the cover zips off, you can wash the items
separately.

- **For a down bed:** Rely on a front-loading washing
machine because a pet bed (like a down comforter)
simply floats in a top-loader and won't get clean. If you
don't have a front-loader, head on over to a friend's
house who has one, brownies (or pet biscuits for a pet
lover) in hand, or go to a Laundromat. Once again, use
1 tablespoon laundry soap and 1 tablespoon oxygen
bleach. Finally, dry this bed in the dryer, again with a
couple of clean tennis balls. If the cover zips off, you can
wash these items separately.

send back new sheets. You spend too much time sleeping to attempt to
rest easy on linens you don't love. I'm convinced that the right sheets
would make the Rosebud Motel (you know, in *Schitt's Creek*) feel like
the Ritz-Carlton.

Changing the sheets might also mean refreshing the look of your bed with a vintage quilt, a handmade coverlet, or a new duvet cover. And keep in mind: You don't have to buy one commercially made. If you or a friend is handy with a sewing machine, you can make your own with a killer fabric remnant. For my masculine bedroom, my duvet is constructed from gray-and-white pinstripe suit material. Or consider adding a fun patchwork or kantha quilt folded lengthwise at the end of your bed for a bright burst of color. A friend of mine uses an oversized needlepoint rug as a coverlet; at night, she simply removes it for sleeping. And then there's Ross, who loves piling blankets on the bed like nobody's business. I get him a new blanket at least once a year.

Here's one more idea. If you sleep with a blanket hog, consider the European approach to bedding: Two twin comforters are used on a queen- or king-size bed—you each get your own. Plus, there's no top sheet, which tends to get tangled around legs anyway. Making such a bed takes about a minute, and sleep is reportedly better without night-

HL Tip: Contrary to popular opinion, mattresses don't double in weight every ten years due to dust mites, dead skin, and oil. It's a myth. However, dust mites, dead skin, and oil *do* accumulate on your sheets. So how often should you wash your bedding? It depends. Here's my rule of thumb: If you wear pajamas and don't lotion-up before bed, wash those sheets once a week. If your pet sleeps on your bed or if you sleep naked, washing your bed linens twice a week is preferred. In fact, if you sleep naked, you probably should stop reading and go wash your sheets right now.

One more note: If you don't have your own laundry room and getting to the Laundromat is a challenge for your busy schedule, keep extra sets of clean bedding on hand and just swap them out.

time wrangling for covers. Finally, during the day, if you don't like the look of two duvets, simply pop a single blanket or quilt over the top of them.

Pillow talk. Queen and king sheet sets come with two pillowcases. But you don't have to stop there. After all, you can never have too many pillows. Sure, you can buy shams that match your bedding, but it's a lot more fun to dress your bed in a variety of pillows. On my bed, for example, I've got a trio of square Euro pillows that lean against the wall, one king-size pillow that rests against that threesome, and two throw pillows grabbing most of the attention up front. It's fun to collect random shams and throw pillows, and it's fairly easy to find a variety on clearance. Or take a methodical approach by selecting perfectly complementary throw pillow covers online. Another thought: If you love monotone bedding, stick with one color, but select pillows in a variety of shades, shapes, sizes, and textures for more interest.

One nightstand. Better yet, two nightstands. So many people keep a plethora of stuff on their nightstand—a lamp, a clock, books and magazines, lotions, medicines, cough drops, a glass of water, a pen or two, earplugs, and more. Unfortunately, that means from the moment you crawl into bed, there's a mess of stuff next to you. Instead, dedicate one drawer in your nightstand to most of these items, keeping them out of sight yet within reach. When I'm reading in bed, I simply open the third drawer in my bureau (which I use as a nightstand), and that gives me easy access to my glasses, tissues, mints to wet my whistle in the middle of the night, and my trusty flashlight for emergencies. When I'm ready for bed, I simply close the drawer.

HL Tip: For a small and/or dark bedroom, consider adding two or three mirrors to the space. The mirrors will not only reflect the light that's in the room but also make your space appear larger.

State of the art. Consider moving your best piece of art to your bedroom. Now hear me out: So many people hang "the good art" in the most public area of the house, likely the living room. But why not feature it in your bedroom?

I remember visiting a client awhile back. She was giving me a tour of her house, and I was stunned when I walked into her bedroom and saw an original Henri Matisse painting. I mean, I'd seen his paintings before but never outside of a museum. When I shared my surprise, especially that it was tucked away in her bedroom, she said simply, "It's my favorite and I want to look at it every morning when I wake up."

Now you and I might not own a Matisse, but it makes sense to keep the artwork that you love most in your sanctum. After all, it's the most personal room in your whole house. Plus, you spend a third of your life in there, so it deserves to feature your fave—whether that's a funky print by your favorite Etsy artist, a *Mona Lisa* poster from the Louvre, an oil painting you found at an estate sale, or whatever you love best. Also, keep in mind: Your art doesn't have to match your duvet—and your bedroom definitely doesn't have to match your house. It's personal.

Out of the blue. Color studies suggest that blue is the best color for a bedroom, leading to more, and more restful, sleep. Plus, blue has the innate ability to lower our heart rates and blood pressure. Who knew?

HL Tip: Think outside the closet for clothing storage. Short on space? Employ vacuumable, space-saving bags under your bed to store off-season clothes. Rather than tuck away ties or scarves, show them off in your bedroom. I use several vintage department-store hooks to hold all my ties. Consider adding a dress form in one corner of your bedroom and outfit it in all your sweaters or jackets.

No wonder it's considered the most relaxing color. Another nature-related color, green, is also a great choice. But either color in a bedroom should be a pale or a deep shade; bright versions of these colors are actually stimulating—in other words, they wake you up.

How could you adopt these colors in your bedroom? Maybe paint your walls blue and add green plants. Or, if you live near the ocean, open your curtains so you can see the blue sea and sky, and then paint your walls green. Or paint three walls white (another restful color) and add blue wallpaper to the fourth wall behind your bed. Or paint all four walls and wallpaper your ceiling!

Need one more reason to paint your bedroom blue? There's an old Southern legend that haints, or evil spirits, avoid water, so painting your spaces blue like water will keep you safe. They even call a certain pale blue-green color *haint blue*. That tradition is why people continue to paint their porch ceilings blue. But why stop there? If there's one place you don't want haints, it's definitely in your bedroom.

Other colors conducive to sleep include soft beige and light pink. Colors deemed too stimulating for the bedroom, at least when used on walls, include bold shades of red, orange, pink, and purple, plus black, dark gray, and brown, which can have a depressive effect on the people who sleep there.

All that said, choose a color you respond to. Back when I worked at high-end department stores, I was constantly surrounded by rich, sumptuous colors, so I chose a more neutral palette at home. These days, without that super-colorful environment, I'm a little more open to adding more colors to my living spaces.

Whatever paint color you choose for your bedroom, be sure to select a flat or matte finish, which diffuses light, helping to create a more restful space.

Closet How-Tos

In terms of rooms, closets are relatively new spaces. It wasn't that long ago—only a couple centuries—that people began to own too many clothes to hang them from wall pegs or in armoires. That's also about the same time that a new invention came about: clothes hangers.

For most of us today, our closets—both reach-in and walk-in—burst with tops and bottoms, shoes and boots, and every possible accessory. Meanwhile, arranging one's closet has become a science, and professional closet installation is an industry.

In the popular sitcom *Modern Family*, the patriarch Jay Pritchett made his fortune designing and manufacturing the almighty closet or, as he described it, "the sanctuary where a man dons his armor in the morning and takes stock of the battle at night!" I'm not so sure about that, but having a well-organized closet goes a long way toward simpler mornings.

While there are lots of suggested rules and regulations for closets, their organization really comes down to common sense and visual order. For example, regarding hangers:

- Use all matching ones; having a mix draws your eyes and your attention away from your clothes. For maximum storage, space efficiency, and staying power, I recommend slim, velvet-covered hangers, which hang on to clothes. (Use these and your favorite shirt won't go missing on the floor of your closet.)
- Hang all of your clothes facing the same direction for easy browsing. Plus, your closet will just look better.
- What should you hang? Dress shirts, blouses, dresses, skirts, dress pants, jackets, and suits stay their best, and nearly wrinkle-free, if they're hung.
- Keep like items together by category—for example, hang all the long-sleeved shirts together and all the pants together.

- Within each category, you can be really extra by hanging your clothes from light to dark or by placing solids with solids and patterned with patterned. You can even hang your clothes by color—not by ROYGBIV, but as retailers do in this order: white, cream, tan, yellow, peach, orange, pink, red, burgundy, powder blue, green, blue, gray, brown, navy blue, and black.

Be imaginative when it comes to clothing and accessory storage. Of course, there are always clear plastic shoe and sweater boxes and wall-mounted wire baskets. But for more environmentally friendly options, consider woven baskets of sustainable materials like palm, rattan, or sisal. You might employ that wine rack or office supplies drawer unit you no longer use for scarves or jewelry, respectively. Or hang your favorite coats or tomorrow's outfit on a dress form. My friend Louise once created a floor-to-ceiling closet shelving unit with boxes tipped on their sides and covered in white Con-Tact paper—brilliant, cheap, and sturdy. It lasted a decade!

Also, don't neglect the brilliance of folding your clothes to maximize closet efficiency. Folding is ideal for sweaters, T-shirts, jeans, lingerie, underwear, and socks. Here are my quick how-tos:

- To fold a shirt, spread it out with the back facing up. Fold in each side to meet the middle and then fold the sleeves down toward the shirt's hem. Now fold the bottom hem to the top and flip the shirt over. If possible, whether you place your shirts in a basket or a drawer, tuck them in vertically, like file folders, to make them more accessible.
- To fold a sweater, again, spread out the garment with its back facing up. Fold in each side to meet the middle and then fold the sleeves down toward the hem. Now fold in thirds. If your dresser can't accommodate all your sweaters, feel free to hang each folded sweater over the bottom rung of a hanger. Hanging a sweater right on a hanger will stretch it out.

- To fold casual pants, place one leg atop the other, fold in half, and then fold in thirds. Like the shirts, line them up in a drawer or basket. If you prefer, you can also hang these pants—folded in half and draped on the bottom rung of a hanger.
- To fold socks, lay one atop the other and roll them up, or fold in halves or thirds for long socks. One trick I'd skip: pulling one sock around the other in a ball—it stretches out the sock.

Be Your Own Guest

When prepping for an overnight visitor, lots of people think ahead, outfitting the guest bedroom with everything Aunt Luna could possibly need. But she comes only one weekend a year, and you live there year-round. Isn't it time to be as considerate of yourself as you would a guest? So, besides making your bed with fresh linens and thoroughly cleaning your room (just like you do before Aunt Luna arrives), what else can you do to treat yourself as a guest? Display a bouquet of your favorite flowers. Introduce a carafe or a vintage pitcher and a glass on your bedside table for late-night sips of water. Add an essential oil diffuser to make your room smell just as lovely as it looks. Indulge in a rich hand cream—a single jar can last many months, so that price tag is a lot smaller than you think. Buy a luxurious new bath towel and perhaps a matching bath mat to dig your toes into—then keep it just for you. And tuck a treat into your bedside drawer—or, better yet, leave it on your pillow.

Trick It Out

With only the addition of a microwave and a mini fridge, I swear I could live in my safari-vibe bedroom. It has everything: my comfy bed, my former kitchen table (now used on the other side of my

HOW TO CLEAN YOUR CLOSET—NOT CLEAN OUT YOUR CLOSET

We've all been there—finally motivated to create those three piles: clothes to keep, clothes to donate, and clothes to throw out or recycle. The next time you're in the thick of this process, pause just long enough to clean that closet before returning that first pile to its hangers. Below are the eight steps that will help make opening your closet and getting dressed a pleasure:

1. Before cleaning inside your closet, grab your 50/50 vinegar-water solution and a cleaning cloth, and wipe down your closet doors.

2. Now open that closet door and replace the light bulb if it's not working.

3. Wax the closet rod, which will allow your clothes hangers to glide with ease. Simply place a piece of wax paper in your hand and slide it over the length of the rod a few times.

4. Get rid of any dry-cleaning bags—instead, if you want to care for out-of-season clothing, drape an old clean sheet (just snip a hole in its middle for the hanger hook) over those clothes, letting them breathe and keeping dust away from your duds.

5. If you haven't already, hang a few cedar blocks from your closet rod. Doing so removes moisture from the air, prevents mildew, keeps away moths, and even adds a pleasant scent to your clothes. By the way, bundles of lavender work just as well—when it comes to clothes,

the French just know. Or use both cedar and lavender, but beware: you'll repel moths but attract suitors.

6. Pull out everything on the floor of your closet and sweep or vacuum. Then straighten all those items as you return them to the closet.

7. Dust anything that requires it—especially that pair of shoes you wear only on your anniversary. Wipe them down. You love those shoes and they deserve respect.

8. Return all your hanging clothes to your closet, ensuring, of course, that everything on the hangers faces in the same direction.

bed), a leather couch, a wingback chair, some greenery in the form of my new favorite plant (a tree fern), and a reproduction woodstove, which reminds me of so many happy memories. Back in the day, my 140-year-old house needed woodstoves; getting out of bed was nearly impossible in otherwise frigid bedrooms. Plus, I'm in Minnesota— she cold.

How else might you spruce up your bedroom and thus simplify your life? Here are a bunch of ideas:

- Do you work in your bedroom? Create a dedicated corner with a small desk and chair, or pair a lounger with a laptop desk and an ottoman with hidden storage. You might also add an under-bed box to hide away work materials, or a room screen that you can set up between your desk and the rest of your bedroom. Being in bed and unable to see your workspace is more conducive to relaxing sleep. (And not being able to see your bed from your workspace may help you resist a midday nap.)

- Like a really clean bedroom? Keep an extra spray bottle of 50/50 vinegar-water solution, a couple of cleaning cloths, and a handheld or stick vacuum tucked in your closet. Then you can clean whenever you get the notion—like a hotel room, which gets refreshed nearly every day.
- Love to read in bed? Then invest in a great reading light. While lots of options exist, I prefer a dimmable, wall-mounted light. Not only does such a sconce mean more real estate on your bedside table, but its swing arm also allows you to focus the light right where you need it or to push it away when you're ready to doze.
- Speaking of dimmers, consider installing a dimmer switch for your overhead light too. With a dimmer, you can lessen the amount of light in the room as you wind down for sleep. I actually recommend dimmers for every room in the house—yes, even the bathroom for mood-lit baths. Plus, these days, you can control dimmer lights via a phone app. In the bedroom, that means you never have to get out of bed to turn off the light.
- Are you like me and dream of a four-poster bed—but don't have the space or the funds? Here's an inexpensive approach: Attach a hook from the ceiling to line up with each of the four corners of your bed; then hang a length of fabric from each hook—an instant four-poster! You can also use this ceiling hook trick to hang Christmas lights all around your bed. Just make sure that you're the one who sparkles brighter.
- If you're a light sleeper, you can rely on a white noise machine to drown out street hubbub, and blackout curtains to keep those REMs revving on bright, sunny mornings. Or for a cheaper approach, buy earplugs and a sleep mask, both of which work surprisingly well.

Time to Clean Up

Keeping in mind that elusive hotel room standard, tending to your bedroom—even if that means just making your bed every morning—should be a priority. Not only does it start your day off right with a small accomplishment, but for many it also leads to less stress, more calm, and better sleep, says Sarah Vanbuskirk ("The Mental Health Benefits of Making Your Bed," *Verywell Mind*, January 29, 2021). And if making your bed does all that, who knows what cleaning your whole bedroom might do? Let's get started.

- To clean your bedroom, like so many other rooms, start at the ceiling, wiping away any cobwebs with a wool duster. Next, turn off your lights and brush off fixtures, including cloth shades, with a horsehair brush. (As always, be sure your lights are off when dusting.) Lastly, check that light bulbs are working and replace as needed.

- Next, strip the bed to wash the sheets and pillowcases. If it's been more than two weeks, consider washing the duvet cover or comforter as well. Drying the sheets with wool balls sprinkled with an essential oil like lavender or peppermint will make crawling back into bed all the sweeter.

- While the bed is bare, take two minutes with your hand vacuum or an attachment to vacuum your mattress—plus any upholstery. (Also, if you find any stains, treat the spots with a horsehair brush, a little laundry soap, and warm water.)

- Before remaking your bed, plump any decorative pillows plus cushions on other bedroom furniture. If you find stains, spot treat or, if covers are removable, remove and wash once a month or so. When they're still damp, right out of the wash, replace them on the cushions and pillows, and stand to dry. Machine-drying may cause shrinkage and make zipping back onto the cushions difficult.

- Before dusting your dresser and any side tables, remove all the items that don't belong—yesterday's coffee mug, a bottle of hair gel, a newspaper, and pens, for example—and return them to where they belong. Now spray a clean terrycloth towel with your 50/50 vinegar-water solution and wipe down your headboard and footboard, side tables, dresser, any glass-fronted art, and windows. If you've got a TV in your bedroom, be sure to wipe the screen and the remotes.
- If you've got a small area rug, roll it up and shake it out in your garbage can or outdoors. If you have a large area rug, simply vacuum. (To actually clean your small or large rug, see "Called on the Carpet" on page 21.)
- Before returning the rugs to a laminate floor, sweep the floor with a stiff corn or straw broom. If the floor is hardwood, use a horsehair broom. If your sealed hardwood floor—it must be sealed— could use more than a quick sweep and you've got a steam cleaner, use that multitasker. Again, caution: Don't use a steam cleaner on

HL Tip: Just like your kiddos and your pets, their toys need a regular bath: To clean plastic toys, place them in the sink and spray them with the 50/50 vinegar-water solution or apply dish soap and water and clean them like you wash the dishes. If you've got toys that are too large to wash in the sink, move this job to the bathtub. Drop a toy on the floor? Don't count on the five-second rule. Instead spray with vodka to sanitize, wait a beat for evaporation, and then you can return the toy to the owner. To clean Teddy and his stuffed pals, simply place them in a mesh bag and wash them in your next load with soap flakes and oxygen bleach. However, if the stuffed animals were made pre-2000, the stuffing isn't machine washable; in that case, spray them with vodka and let them dry.

an unsealed wood floor or an engineered floor; a steam cleaner can damage both types.

- If you've got wall-to-wall carpet or a large area rug, get vacuuming after first picking up any bobby pins, wrappers, coins, etc. Even one doodad can cause issues for a vacuum. And don't discount the power of the crevice tool to suck up dust and dirt from room corners, ceiling corners, sofa cushions, bookcases, and more.

- Throw dirty clothes in the hamper, return clean clothes to your dresser and closet, and close that closet door. (For tips on cleaning the closet, see "How to Clean Your Closet—Not Clean Out Your Closet" on page 104.)

- Last, straighten any stacks of books and magazines, donating or recycling those you no longer want. Organize items that belong on your bedside tables and dresser, and empty the trash can.

- Now it's time for a nap—fortunately, your perfectly made bed with its clean bed linens is waiting!

The Ten-Minute Clean: Bedroom

Your oldest friends and tonight's dinner guests have just voiced interest in touring your whole house. It's their first visit and they won't be swayed—they want to see every room. While they dally over dessert, you excuse yourself for ten minutes, all the time you need to make your bedroom look fantastic.

- Light one lamp—if the rest are dusty, they'll never know.
- Make your bed, plump the pillows, and refold your throw.
- Organize any items on your bedside tables and dresser.
- Gather up any glasses and mugs, and set them by the bedroom door to take with you back to the kitchen.
- Straighten your stack of reading materials.
- Plump any pillows on a love seat or chair.
- Throw dirty clothes in the hamper.
- Stuff any clean clothes, shoes, belts, etc., inside the closet and close the door.

- Return to your guests (after dropping off those glasses and mugs) and lead them on the tour, perhaps with glasses of wine in hand.

My Ten-Minute Cleaning Playlist: Bedroom (Upbeat)
- "Dress You Up" by Madonna (3:38)
- "Just Like Heaven" by the Cure (3:32)
- "So What" by Pink (3:35)

My Ten-Minute Cleaning Playlist: Bedroom (Mellow)
- "The Winner Takes It All" by ABBA (4:55)
- "Sittin' Up in My Room" by Brandy (4:51)

HELPING YOUR KID CLEAN THEIR ROOM

From the time a child is about two years old, they can likely join in the fun of cleaning up the house, whether carrying their own cup to the sink or plunking their favorite stuffed animal on the bed. A friend of a friend used to invite his kiddos to pick up whatever they could in their bedrooms before the end of three fun songs, dancing a bit while they straightened. There was no pressure to make everything look perfect—just a fun family dance party with some cleaning thrown in for good measure. I love that approach to teaching kids about caring for their home!

I also sign on to the theory that cleaning your own space isn't a family chore. A family chore is, for example, dusting the living room or cleaning the bathroom or taking out the garbage—a task that helps everyone in the family. A child cleaning their own bedroom might make parents feel better when they peek in the door, but the child is really the beneficiary.

What follows is one step-by-step cleaning approach—there are lots—for a child, roughly aged seven to twelve. I borrowed it from a friend of mine. I hope it's helpful! For some children, it might take ten minutes; for others, it might take an hour. If it's too much for your kid, don't sweat it. Every child develops individually, and this method might be good to try again down the road.

1.   Turn on some fun music or an audiobook to listen to while you pick up your room. Maybe someone is helping you clean, or maybe you're doing this on your own. Either way, good for you!

2. Next, straighten your duvet and put your pillow where it belongs. Easy! If you keep your stuffed animals on your bed, arrange them on your bed too.

3. Now here's the real trick to cleaning your room: Pick up everything off the floor that doesn't belong there and place it on your bed. "Whoa!" you're saying. "Now my bed is messy again." That's okay—it won't be for long. Sometimes things have to get a bit messier before they can get neater. After all, check out your floor—it's already looking so much better!

    - Now, take all the dirty clothes off your bed and place them in the hamper.
    - Next, return any clean clothes to your closet or dresser.
    - Now, remove all the books from your bed and place them back where they belong.
    - Next, return toys to where they belong—for example, place Legos in a Lego container.
    - Is there anything left on the bed that doesn't belong there? If yes, put it away.

4. Now look under all the furniture in your room—your bed, a desk, a chair, maybe a dresser. If you find any treasures, return them to wherever they belong.

5. Your room probably looks pretty awesome by now. Fantastic—you're done! (And if it doesn't look quite awesome, no biggie. What's one more thing that you can do to make it look even better?)

6. Give a little yell—"Hooray!"—you did it!

CHAPTER 6

BATHROOM
TOTALLY (RUBBER) DUCKY

Anyone who thinks heaven is not hot water behind a locked door has forgotten what it means to live.

—Lucy Frank, *Two Girls Staring at the Ceiling*

Lounging in a hot bath may seem like the height of luxury and a relatively modern indulgence, what with the proliferation of bath bombs, bath oils, bath salts, bath pillows, and bath mats. Oh, and let's not forget the revelatory bath tray, which simultaneously keeps your book dry and your wineglass handy.

But think again: Luxuriating in a bath goes back thousands of years. How do I know? Frankly, I'm a bathing expert—in fact, I take a bath every day, just like the ancient Romans. But my bathing ritual pales in comparison to theirs.

Those Romans, from all walks of life, really knew how to bathe. First, they'd oil up their bodies to loosen the dirt accumulated during their workday. Then they'd exercise in a palaestra, basically a gym, working up a sweat before scraping off all that oil, perspiration, and dirt with a handheld metal tool called a strigil. Next came the fun part: moving—often via tunnels—from room to room, including the oleoterion (massage room), the laconicum (sauna), the caldarium (hot bath), the tepidarium (lukewarm bath), and the frigidarium (cold bath). This practice could take hours.

Throughout this process, they hung out with friends, held business meetings, got their makeup done (with cosmetics made from charcoal, ground oyster shells, honey, rose petals, and more), got their hair tweezed (both women and men), and even dined on take-out food. For bathers at more expansive facilities, they might have whiled away their afternoons in additional rooms, including a solarium (sunbathing room), a sudatorium (steam room), a library, a reading room, a lecture hall, and more. All this complexity makes our bathing routines—even those of the most privileged among us—sound pretty basic, huh?

But wait—there's more: The largest and most elaborate Roman baths accommodated thousands of people and featured high ceilings, large windows, extravagant frescoes and mosaics, bronze and silver faucets, outdoor swimming pools, and enormous gardens with statuary and fountains. I marvel when I realize that all this was built two thousand years ago. Sounds like a place you'd like to go? Me too.

Of course, all of this activity was communal. Today, most of us prefer to do our bathing in private, but we still want our bathrooms to be places of rest, relaxation, and rejuvenation. And that's why we can take our inspiration from the ancient Romans.

Getting Inspired

For the first bathroom I ever decorated, I had some of the Roman ideas in mind—on a minuscule scale. The room had a sixty-inch cast-iron bathtub, one window, and little storage. In contrast to the Key lime palette I used throughout the rest of my apartment, I painted this bathroom a rusty orange, hung a flowerpot on a wrought-iron hanger to hold all of my toiletries, and sewed a wall-to-wall and floor-to-ceiling shower curtain from inexpensive muslin, which I tied back with a black ribbon whenever needed. Truly, taking a bath in that enclosed space felt like stepping into a caldarium.

Today, my bathroom differs greatly from that one twenty years ago, although I still have a claw-foot tub—this one is original to our building and seventy-two inches long. The tub's interior is white, but its exterior is painted green-gray to match our slate shower tile. The rest of our fixtures are white as well, plus we have white wooden shutters to spruce up the window, and the ceiling and trim are painted a white semigloss. A silver lamé shower curtain adds a splash of bling.

The space is beautiful, but it's one of two rooms in our house I have regrets about. I should have added a heated floor in our entryway, and I should have created the bathroom I'd dreamed of for years. My vision? To install a black-and-white hexagonal tiled floor; to add white tile up the walls to picture-rail height of roughly seven feet; to apply Martinique, the banana-leaf wallpaper made famous by the Beverly Hills Hotel, above the tile; and to paint the ceiling blue. The tile would have been period correct for our neoclassical home, and that wallpaper would have been a likely choice for someone remodeling our house back in the 1940s. In addition to those changes, I would've swapped the shower and commode locations.

Why didn't I follow through? After purchasing our home, we spent a summer remodeling before moving in, but we ran out of time to source everything, so I gave up on these changes. Still, I wish I'd gone with my gut. Given the chance for a do-over, I'd also install floor heating in the shower and create a wet room, adding a divider between the tub and shower and the rest of the room.

Is there anything about your bathroom (or bathrooms) you'd like to change? Or perhaps many things, like me? If so, where do you find your inspiration? In addition to recognizing the genius of those venerable Romans, I often find insights in restaurant bathrooms. Now, bear with me—no, not those washrooms found down long, dark hallways or those generic lavatories located at the back of fast-food joints. I'm talking about beautiful, thoughtfully designed bathrooms created by people who want the entire experience of visiting their restaurants to be wonderfully memorable.

Have you ever been dining out when a friend returns to the table and announces, "You've got to go see the bathroom!" That's what

HL Tip: Yes, adding lavender to your bath is a lovely way to prepare for sleep. But how can you oomph your morning shower to prepare for the day ahead? Just add two or three drops of a citrus essential oil—clementine, grapefruit, orange, or tangerine (or mix a couple)—onto the floor of your shower. Turn on the warm water for a few seconds and then step in. The energizing scent will start your day off right. (If you're stuffy, use eucalyptus oil. Or tie a bunch of eucalyptus to your showerhead. That's what I do all winter long.)

I'm talking about: places like the century-old Drake Hotel in Chicago, whose lush, garden-themed Palm Court ladies' room features private suites with personal makeup tables; the Ivy, a high-tea destination in Bath, England, whose bathroom ceiling is richly festooned with silk flowers; or Buca di Beppo, a kitschy Italian restaurant chain whose men's bathroom walls are covered in pictures of Roman water fountains. They make me laugh every time I'm there.

In fact, many of the ideas I wish I'd implemented in my bathroom were inspired by a palatial old house and special-events venue in Shelbyville, Kentucky. For a while, I co-owned a floral-events service, and I was lucky enough to design flowers for a few weddings there. Tucked under its grand staircase were two powder rooms. The men's (I never did pop my head into the women's) featured a black-and-white-tiled floor and sheets of marble up the walls to picture-rail height. It was such a beautiful and easy-to-clean design choice that I never forgot it. Plus, above the tile, the walls were painted burgundy—adding personality via color.

I asked my coauthor, Karin, about her favorite public bathroom and she vividly remembers being gobsmacked as a child when she visited the twelfth-floor women's lounge at Dayton's, a former department store in Minneapolis. As Karin walked in, she discovered a red-carpeted hallway lined with mirrored makeup tables and upholstered chairs on which beautiful women were powdering their noses. (It brings to mind that dressing room scene in the 1939 film *The Women*.)

HL Tip: When you find a towel you love, load up. Then as you wash, dry, and put towels away, rotate them, placing the newly cleaned ones on the bottom of the stack, so your towels wear evenly. No one wants to use that one towel that's showing more wear and tear than the others.

Beyond the hallway, she entered a round, mirrored room—with sinks all around and a chandelier overhead. Like she said, as a little kid, she was gobsmacked. And this was after walking through a grand department store. It's no wonder then that when it came time to decorate her bathroom, she added a decidedly feminine flair.

Can you recall a public bathroom that felt serene? Or made you feel pampered? Or made you laugh? How might that space influence your design choices now?

Time to Freshen Up

There are so many ways you can update your bathroom without ever dipping into your 401(k), grabbing your sledgehammer, or donning some painting overalls. In fact, you can update your bathroom in a single day or less with one or more of the ideas that follow.

Looking good. In your living room, it's unlikely that you've hung a painting of a couch or a chair. In your kitchen, there's probably not a print of a stove or a refrigerator. Same goes for a bedroom—there's likely no bed photo hanging over your bed. And yet bathroom art tends to feature water—people bathing, animals bathing, even rubber duckies bathing. You get the picture. And let's not even get started talking about toilet art. Or framed potty sayings as art. (No, thank you.)

Instead, let's expand our horizons. Perhaps the art you use to refresh your bathroom is only peripherally water-related—an acrylic beach painting, a photo of synchronized swimmers, or a whimsical mermaid watercolor. Or maybe you leave the theme of water behind and select art based on a hobby, say a peacock print if you're a bird lover, framed buttons if you like to sew, or a concert poster if you're a drummer. One nature-loving friend has hung a giant photo of a leaf in her powder room—the size of the frame is both surprising and sophisticated.

In contrast, rather than traditional art, you might hang woven baskets or vintage hats. In my bathroom, I've got an antique wrought-iron gate hanging for most of the year on my one available wall. In the winter, I switch it up with a feathered wreath.

Or maybe you love being surrounded by your favorite travel-related souvenirs. In a friend's bathroom, she's hung a colorful island print purchased on a cruise plus a whimsical angel head made from a coconut shell in Guerrero, Mexico.

Or consider hanging a quote that inspires you, motivates you, or makes you laugh. I love pretty much anything that Oscar Wilde ever wrote, for example: "I can resist anything except temptation." Or how about framing a Mindy Kaling quote from her hilarious and honest memoir *Is Everyone Hanging Out Without Me?*: "Sometimes you just have to put on lip gloss and pretend to be psyched." What's your favorite quote? I bet it would look great framed.

And speaking of frames, both metal and wood ones work just fine in the humid surrounds of a bathroom. Just be sure to protect your art by having it sealed on the back (professional framers always do this) and use your exhaust fan or open the windows during showers and baths.

Pushing daisies. Introducing a single philodendron plant or a virtual jungle to your bathroom looks great and literally adds life to your space. Plus, plants create more oxygen for you to breathe via photosynthesis and help purify your air, absorbing other gases and airborne toxins through phytoremediation, transpiration, and stomata—all related processes.

Need another reason to add a plant to your bathroom? Plants are scientifically proven to boost positive emotions and decrease negative ones. Spending time in a room with plants can actually make you feel "happier and more satisfied . . . more peaceful and positive," says Lala Tanmoy Das ("What Science Tells Us About the Mood-Boosting Effects of Indoor Plants," *The Washington Post*, June 7, 2022).

As you select plants, consider your bathroom's light, humidity, and fluctuating temperatures:

- If your bathroom is full of natural light, you're lucky. Bathrooms can often be dark, making it important to choose plants that thrive in low light. A friend whose bathroom lacked any window at all added a tubular skylight capped by a small rooftop dome. Now natural light pours into the space and her plants thrive.

- Not all plants do well with humidity—cacti and certain succulents aren't good choices, for example.
- If you live in a cold climate, that monstera and gardenia might not make great choices either. Sure, they're happy as can be when you're enjoying a steamy shower in the morning, but those chilly temps won't suit them at all overnight.
- Which plants are you safe selecting? I'd suggest begonias, Chinese evergreens, leopard lilies (*Dieffenbachia*), ferns like lemon button and Japanese holly, philodendrons, parlor palms, and ZZ plants.

In my bathroom during the winter, I keep my pride and joy, a lime tree I named Brian Jones after the fashionable founder of the Rolling Stones. Plus, it's fun to live in the north and have a lime tree. He sits out on our sunny deck all summer and then retreats to our bathroom the rest of the year. And, yes, I get to harvest a lime or two a few times a year; I use them in my gin and tonics. (My ultimate desire? To have an orangery—a fancy greenhouse added on to my house that would let me grow and harvest all kinds of citrus fruits plus tomatoes year-round.)

Creating a soft spot. Bathrooms tend to be full of hard surfaces—mirrors, countertops, cabinets, tiled walls and floors and, of course, bathtubs and toilets. To soften up your bathroom, you can stock it with thirsty towels, of course, but what else? Rather than a vinyl shower curtain, consider having one made of fabric, either ready-made or one you've made yourself. Natural fabrics—like cotton, linen, and hemp—offer a sophisticated look and are easy to wash. Just use a high-quality shower-curtain liner. And speaking of curtains, the same natural fabrics look lovely as bathroom window curtains. More softening ideas include topping a bathroom stool with a terrycloth pillow or cushion, adding a textile wall hanging to the room, suspending a plant in a crocheted hanger made for that purpose, or adding a small pouf for a seat.

As for rugs, don't feel hemmed in by fluffy monotone bath mats, although their rubber backings make them smart choices. Bath rugs today come in every fabric—from cotton to sisal to wool (yes, wool works great in the bathroom); every color—from whites, grays, and pastels to brilliant bold and colorful neons; every shape—from rectangle, round, and oval to floral, emblematic, and animal hide; and every style, including Oriental, Persian, patterned, and overdyed. Some are textured or tufted, feature pom-poms or tassels, or are even reversible. Got company coming? Flip that reversible rug over to its unused, pristine side, and no one will be the wiser. Keep in mind: You can use any rug in a bathroom; just be sure to place a nonslip pad beneath it if it doesn't have a rubber backing.

Going full-on spa. If you're not enjoying your bathroom, something is off. A modern bathroom, after all, is designed for "me time." Like I said, I take a bath every night. Most nights it's a twenty-minute affair with lavender-scented Epsom salts. They put me in the mood for sleep so I can drift off as soon as I crawl under my black cotton sheets. (No, despite what it says in *Laundry Love*, I don't sleep on black satin— truthfully, I'm just not that interesting.)

Thanks to my waterproof smartphone (an absolute must for a professional laundry dude), I catch up on social media, read the newspaper, or flip through a favorite magazine while I'm soaking. Other times I just think—I often get my best ideas in the bath. Depending on the night, I may be sipping hot tea or a cold cocktail. I have even, on occasion, enjoyed a facial.

How do you treat yourself in the bathroom? And I do mean treat yourself. The more hectic, busy, or chaotic your life is, the more important it is to take time for you. Splurging on yourself with a few special products in your bathroom can make a huge difference as you get ready in the morning or wrap up your day before sleep. They can also make your bathroom feel serene, even like you're at a spa.

To really get the look, consider tucking away extraneous items so your countertop stars a lovely hand soap, a rich body cream, and a scented candle. Then, in the bathtub or shower, rather than display a hodgepodge of products, buy your body wash, shampoo, and conditioner from the same line. Spas, for example, almost always use one line of products. A friend takes this idea one step further, matching her family's two bathrooms—one green and blue, the other pink and gray—to bath brands whose packaging coordinates with each bathroom. That may sound over the top, but the color coordination only adds to the tranquil look.

How else might you make your bathroom seem more like a spa? You don't need to purchase caviar-infused eye cream and facial serums flecked with 24-karat gold—unless you want to. But perhaps you feel wonderful whenever you spritz your hair with rose-infused spray, treat your face to a manuka oil facial mask, remove your makeup with cold-pressed camellia oil, or shave your beard with a patchouli-scented shaving cream. Whatever you choose—peels, exfoliants, creams, polishes, oils, butters, or scrubs be sure it's something that makes you feel special.

Even brushing your teeth can boost your mood. I already mentioned my love for Crabtree & Evelyn toothpaste back when that was a thing. Today, my go-to is Marvis, the beloved Italian toothpaste brand known for its intense flavors like aquatic mint, ginger mint, and Amarelli licorice. But there are plenty of other luxurious toothpastes, including Linhart with its signature minty anise flavor and Opiat Dentaire in orange-ginger-clove. A 3.4-ounce tube typically lasts well over a month, so fifteen bucks isn't too crazy indulgent. Besides, a fun flavor just might have you brushing better and more often.

The same holds true for floss. Given plain-Jane, no-flavor string or, worse, floss that tastes like pickles (yes, some minty floss tastes strongly of dill), most people do the deed just once or twice a week. (Granny Dude would be horrified.) I vote for fun-flavored floss any day—orange, strawberry, or coconut, anyone? Or take better care of the planet and buy compostable bamboo floss.

Ah, the Linen Closet

Just saying the phrase *linen closet* aloud elevates my home, even if it's momentarily messy. Having a linen closet means you've got linens—bedding and towels—that are cleaned, pressed (maybe!), folded, and awaiting use by a guest or, better yet, you. The sheer luxury of it all!

But you don't have to stop there. A linen closet is a great place to store items that your household members share: the iron and ironing board, extra pillows, extra blankets for chilly nights or spontaneous kid sleepovers, a fan, a humidifier, a heating pad, a neck massager, even essential oils. If you've got the space, other items to store in the linen closet, particularly if it's close to your sleeping space, include boxes of tissue, lotion, light bulbs for lights on that floor, extra batteries for your bedside flashlight, a lint brush if Lexi sleeps on your bed, a couple of extra microfiber cloths, and a spray bottle of 50/50 vinegar-water solution.

Finally, the linen closet is the perfect place to use shelf liners, to tuck sachets in between towels or sheets, and to hide candy on the top shelf. (Note: This last tip doesn't work if you share your household with someone who is taller than you.)

HL Tip: Need to reorganize your linen closet? A good first step is clearing out old, faded towels and bedding that you know (deep down) you'll never use again. But don't throw them away. Rip up the old towels and use them as cleaning cloths. Or use old towels to wipe off Rumi's paws and belly on muddy spring and fall days. Or donate used towels and bedding to a local humane society, animal rescue organization, or veterinarian, any of which can use them to care for pets. Just call ahead before donating.

Time to Clean Up

Welcome to the bathroom, the second-germiest room in the house. The kitchen is the big winner, but this room too can offer a pile of viruses and a bevy of bacteria—stuff like *Campylobacter*, *Escherichia coli* (*E. coli*), and *Streptococcus*. Not good. We don't need to go into all the deets, but just know this stuff can make you sick. Understanding this is likely all the motivation you need to get cleaning. Need one more reason? Getting yourself clean in a bathroom that's clean just makes sense.

- For some real peace and quiet, tell anyone who lives with you that you're going to clean the bathroom. It's highly unlikely they'll offer to help after that announcement. Trust me—this is going to be good.
- Now spray the mirror with the 50/50 vinegar-water solution, wiping away hairspray, shaving cream, and more. (Perhaps you need to remove a note in lipstick left on the mirror à la Elizabeth Taylor in *BUtterfield 8* or Cam in *Modern Family*. By the way, more than a few people have compared me to Cam—I take that as a huge compliment.) Be sure also to wipe the area between the mirror and the

HL Tip: Rather than buy plastic containers designed for your medicine cabinet, consider using ramekins. I use a bunch in my cabinet, dedicating each to a different item: swabs, cotton balls (or reusable cotton cloth rounds), tweezers, and more. Or use baby food jars, garlic jars, or juice glasses. You can even label the contents—say, safety pins—with etching cream. Best of all, just throw them in the dishwasher when they need cleaning.

FIVE CLEVER TOILET-CLEANING TRICKS

1. If you have hard water and tend to get lime stains in the toilet bowl, place special toilet magnets (chemical free!) into the tank to attract all those minerals, preventing stains in your toilet bowl from ever appearing again. (Every so often, take them out and wipe off.)

2. If you're cleaning elsewhere in the house with a solution of water and sodium percarbonate and you've got some remaining solution, simply pour into the toilet and scrub with the toilet brush. Why skip out on an extra-clean commode?

3. To empty out the toilet so you can really get at those stains with a brush, pour a bucket of water in one swoosh into the bowl; the toilet will self-flush. Now scrub and flush again, and the toilet will refill.

4. Here's another trick: Dump 1 cup of vinegar into the toilet bowl and then add 1 cup of baking soda. More than that famous volcano on *The Brady Bunch*, this acid-plus-base antibacterial approach will get your bowl squeaky clean—just add the scrub brush and a bit of muscle. Then rinse by flushing.

5. Here's my final and perhaps best toilet-cleaning trick: Replace your standard toilet seat with a quick-release version for about twenty bucks. From now on, just pop the seat off the commode and spray or steam clean it in the bathtub. Meanwhile, the rest of the toilet will be far easier to clean as well. No lie: This will change your bathroom-cleaning life.

countertop, which often has blotches of makeup and toothpaste. And if it's been a while, remove everything from your bathroom cabinet, spray the shelves with the vinegar solution, wipe dry, and return the items (reorganizing as you go and recycling empty containers).

- Look up at the light fixture. With the light off, dust it with a feather duster and even give the light bulbs a swoosh.

- Clear the counter, tucking away any unneeded items under the sink or in the linen closet. (Why do I have three half-empty bottles of hair gel?) Now use a dollop of dish soap on a damp washcloth to wipe down the counter and the sink. You just don't need all those chemicals. Dish soap is enough. Why do I say never to use dish soap when you're washing clothes but recommend it for cleaning the sink, tub, and more in the bathroom? Chemistry, my friend. Thanks to its acidity, dish soap is designed to cut the grease. For clothing, dish soap is thus much too harsh, but think about the sink and tub and all those oily products—creams, conditioners, moisturizers, and more—that we use in these spaces. That's exactly why dish soap works so well. And so, if the sink is particularly dirty, add the stopper to the drain, run some water in there and add a dot or two of dish soap. Then use a towel to give that sink a deeper scrub. And give that faucet a polish as well— everything looks so much better when stainless shines.

- Next up is the tub—simply pick your adventure: One, if you're my mom and you clean the tub three times a week, all you need is the vinegar-water solution—just spray and wipe dry. Two, if your tub gets a good cleaning once a week or so, add dish soap to a damp cloth and use some elbow grease. And three, if you've got hard-water spots, soap crayons, residue from bath bombs, and more, it's time to pull out the steamer or the orbital buffer. (See page xxii for tips on steaming.) If you use the buffer, apply some dish soap to your cleaning pad and buff away all those spots and more. Then just rinse the tub.

- Someone has got to clean the commode. Just remember that you're cleaning it for you and everyone who lives with you. First, spray the exterior with the vinegar solution and wipe. Then, drip a drop or two of dish soap into the toilet, scrub with the toilet brush, give it a flush, and you're good to go—literally. For a deeper clean, every so often, use the steam cleaner on the outside. The first time I did this, I was equally horrified at the who-knows-what dripping off the porcelain (have a rag handy) and thrilled at how clean the toilet became.

- Next, remove any used towels from the floor plus the bathroom rug and place into the hamper. Now, for a fast clean floor, simply spray with the vinegar solution and wipe with a towel. If your floor deserves a bit more attention, use the dish soap and damp towel approach. But if your floor cries out for major cleaning, pull out that steam cleaner, which works like nobody's business to sanitize, deodorize, and clean your floor. Even your lint—gone!

- And now here's a message to take care of your walls. Every once in a while (but not every week), use a damp terrycloth towel or a microfiber mop to wipe down your walls, top to bottom. If you really want to go all out you can even vacuum them, but that's probably not necessary.

- Use a microfiber cloth (a large one for car detailing works great) to clean chrome towel bars, the toilet paper holder, the trash can, and more.

- Finally, water any plant that needs it, flip the sticks in your essential oil diffuser, replace the towels and toilet paper roll if needed, empty the garbage can, and place a clean rug on the floor (making sure it covers that one annoying cracked tile).

- Now, since everyone still thinks you're cleaning the bathroom, take this opportunity to enjoy a long luxurious bath. Just pull out the chilled wine you stashed in your cleaning bucket, light a candle, and you're ready. After all, from the tub is the perfect spot to admire your work.

SIX ITEMS TO MAKE YOUR HOTEL BATHROOM MORE LUXURIOUS

1. **A super plush bathrobe.** If you know that your hotel isn't the type to supply a dual-layer, all-cotton, long-loop terry robe, pack your favorite or treat yourself to a new one in honor of your trip.

2. **Bath oils, salts, and/or bombs.** A relaxing bath after hours of sightseeing or working all day can get you in the mood for sleep in a new place. Bring along your favorites or buy a new scent once you arrive.

3. **A deluxe face and/or hair mask.** You want to look your best while traveling, so don't hold back on the pampering. One caveat: Now's the time for a tried-and-true brand. Experimenting with a new one might not be the best idea, especially if you have sensitive skin.

4. **A heavenly travel candle.** Typically packed in a tin and offering just enough wax for a week or so of lightings, a travel candle (or two) adds instant atmosphere. (Don't forget the matches.)

5. **Your trusty smartphone.** Skip "Baby Shark" and "Rubber Duckie" (even Daveed Diggs's version), and select the bath-time music you love best—perhaps a spa playlist, nature sounds, or the soundtrack to *Pride & Prejudice*.

6. **And, surprise, hotel shampoo.** If you feel uncertain about the chemicals used to clean the bathtub (and don't want them mixing with your bathwater), give that tub a quick wipe-down with a washcloth and a dollop of shampoo from that tiny bottle left for you.

The Ten-Minute Clean: Bathroom

Your old friend, in from out of town, just texted: "Are we still on for drinks tonight?" You text back: "Of course! See you at 7." And then you panic. You completely forgot about your invitation—until now. You've got plenty of drinks and snacks on hand. What you don't have? A clean bathroom. No worries. You can do this in less than ten minutes. And if we're talking a powder room, you'll be sitting pretty in less than five. Now let's get going!

- First, spray the mirror with the 50/50 vinegar-water solution and wipe it down. Once the mirror is clean, everything will look better.
- Now turn off the lights and wipe the light bulbs—doing so only takes seconds but will make a big difference in the look of your bathroom.
- Clear the counter, tucking away any unneeded items under the sink or in the linen closet. (Wait—do I have another bottle of hair gel?) Now use a dot of dish soap on a damp washcloth to wipe down the counter and the sink. And don't neglect the faucet.
- Throw any used towels into the hamper or the bathtub. Now just pull that shower curtain closed—out of sight, out of mind. Especially if you're expecting guests, there's no need for them to look beyond the curtain. (The wizard isn't back there.)
- Next, clean the commode—you and any visitors deserve a clean one. Spray the exterior with the vinegar solution and wipe down the seat and sides. Drip a drop or two of dish soap into the toilet, scrub with the toilet brush, and give it a flush.
- Sweep the floor or just wipe up the obvious areas that need it with the washcloth.
- Now for the accessories: Turn any plant so its best side is showing, flip the sticks in your essential oil diffuser, replace the hand towel, empty the garbage can, and make sure that the toilet paper roll isn't on its last few squares. (It should be pleasantly plump.)
- Take a deep cleaning breath. You're ready.

My Ten-Minute Cleaning Playlist: Bathroom (Upbeat)

- "Crazy in Love" by Beyoncé (3:56)
- "Chains of Love" by Erasure (3:46)
- "9 to 5" by Dolly Parton (2:46)

My Ten-Minute Cleaning Playlist: Bathroom (Mellow)

- "Where Did Our Love Go" by the Supremes (2:39)
- "Angel of Harlem" by U2 (3:48)
- "(Forever) Live and Die" by OMD (3:35)

HL Tip: This is an old tip but a good one. If you've washed and dried a set of sheets that you plan to tuck into the linen closet, here's what you do: Make a stack with the bottom sheet, the flat sheet, and one pillowcase. Then slide this stack into the second pillowcase. (If the sheet set is for a twin bed, just slide the folded bottom sheet and flat sheet into the one pillowcase.) That way, they're all together and ready to be placed on a bed—you don't have to rummage through a stack to find what you need. If you're super fancy, tie up the pillowcase with a grosgrain ribbon so the sheets inside don't slide. (I know you're thinking: "I'd love to do that, but who has the time?" Me too, but, boy, I really love grosgrain ribbon.)

CHAPTER 7

LAUNDRY ROOM
BREATHING ROOM

The laundry room—it's simply the greatest room in the house.

—Patric Richardson

U p until this chapter, we haven't focused on a space that exists simply because of chores. We might clean the living room, but that's not its purpose. Same goes for the dining room. Even the kitchen is a place where people both eat and cook—something that brings lots of us joy.

But the laundry room revolves around chores—washing textiles, drying them, ironing them, and much more. Many people enjoy doing laundry, including yours truly. I've loved doing laundry since I was three years old, helping Granny Dude hang the wash on the clothesline. I even got a toy washing machine that year from Santa. I understood from a young age that doing laundry for your family was a gift.

Yet the majority of people view laundry as their least favorite task—study after study confirms this. (Of course, most of those studies predated the publication of *Laundry Love*, which has the power to change this attitude, but I digress.)

Here's my take on this laundry cycle:

1. If you hate doing laundry
2. and your laundry room is dark, depressing, or both,
3. then you'll procrastinate doing laundry,
4. your laundry will pile up,
5. and you'll hate doing laundry even more.

This chapter aims to end that for those who hate laundry. And for those who love laundry, I offer loads of ways to transform or refresh your laundry room as well.

Getting Inspired

Because I enjoy laundry and because I'm known as the Laundry Evangelist (and also the Laundry Guy, take your pick), you might assume my laundry room is tricked out with multiple washers and dryers for efficiency, a steam cabinet for professional steaming, built-in wooden racks for air-drying, a jetted laundry sink for handwashing, bright lighting for stain removal, an ironing board with a mangle (a large ironing machine) at the ready, an oversized island for clothes folding, a wool ball dispenser (plus a rack of essential oils), and a mini fridge for both kinds of vodka—laundry and drinking. (And of course, a disco ball.)

If you've read *Laundry Love*, many of these amenities might sound familiar, but then you also know the truth: I have a combination bathroom/laundry room, and the washer and dryer are just steps from my bathtub. Only a few of those aforementioned niceties are part of my laundry setup. But that's okay.

I count myself lucky to do laundry in a bright, sunny space, since most of us inherit our laundry rooms from previous homeowners. If we're lucky enough to have laundry facilities at all, they're commonly found in a dark basement with only a glint of light from a single hopper window. But that doesn't mean we must settle. It only makes sense that having a functional and good-looking laundry room inspires more and better laundry sessions.

Before we get started, however, I must add one more feature to my dream laundry room. After touring the historic James J. Hill House, the largest (thirty-six thousand square feet) and most expensive home in Minnesota at roughly one million dollars back when it was completed in 1891, I've decided I too need a bluing sink. Next to a disco ball and a mangle, this seems like a must.

I'd never even heard of a dedicated bluing sink until my visit. During the turn of the last century, laundry was a laborious process with a capital *L*, and maintaining white clothing and textiles was a daunting challenge. That was likely especially true at the grandest home in Minnesota, what with the hundreds of napkins, dozens of tablecloths, and piles of bedclothes. Not to mention Mr. Hill's white shirts. There could've been no ring around the collar or yellowing for the Empire Builder.

HL Tip: While so many laundry rooms feature a wall of cabinets, you can survive without them. What you do need, however, is a rod on which to hang a bunch of hangers and all those wet clothes to air-dry. If you've got the room, a hanging rod might just be the best thing you can possibly add to your laundry room beyond the washer and dryer. Or if you only have a little room, consider installing a Sheila Maid, the Victorian-styled "clothes airer" that lowers from the ceiling by pulley and then can be lifted out of the way when not in use. If you have next to no room, simply add a few hooks to the ceiling or the rafters from which to hang some hangers.

Fortunately, bluing—made mostly of blue pigment and water—was and is an inexpensive, nontoxic, and biodegradable liquid that home-makers could add to their wash. Just a few drops added to the wash water would bring back the original color to their white garments, sheets, and towels. That's because adding microscopic blue particles to white fabric causes it to reflect more light and look whiter.

For the wealthy Hills, their household staff took care of all that white laundry, likely following that era's prescriptive thirteen-step process: soaking, washing, rinsing, boiling, rinsing again, bluing, starching, hanging, drying, sprinkling, stretching, ironing, and folding. Phew! Today, it's just a matter of adding oxygen bleach to your laundry soap and you're practically golden.

Hill staffers might've counted themselves lucky to work in a laundry room that remains impressive even by today's standards. Its square footage likely matches that of my entire house. And its features include eighteen racks made of cedar (with its moth-repellant properties) upon which to hang wet clothes, plus a cabinet for tucking away those racks; radiator pipes over which wet clothes dried overnight; and four giant tubs (with wood surrounds and turned legs)—a washing tub, a rinsing tub, that fabulous bluing tub, and one more tub for good measure (maybe for a quick foot soak between loads?).

Whether your laundry room is on par with the Hills', a simple closet with a stacked washer and dryer, a dingy basement space with horror-flick overtones, a mudroom- or bathroom-laundry combo, or even a corner in your garage, you can always boost the look and feel of your space. (That said, if your laundry room is a magazine-spread-worthy affair with a potting table, gift wrap center, dog wash station, and small dance floor beneath your disco ball, please invite me over.)

Time to Freshen Up

When I was a kid, our basement laundry room was my boy cave. When it was cold or rainy or a hundred degrees outside, I could hang out there. The laundry room was always comfortable and comforting—there was the white noise hum of the washer and dryer, the perfectly consistent basement temperature, and plenty of alone space and time for doing laundry, watching TV, or making crafts. (If it's a craft, I've done it at least once.)

That's what I wish for you: a transformation of this tireless space to elevate your laundry tasks. This room likely sees you a considerable amount of time. Refreshing the space via greater organization and new ideas will make the time that you spend there all the better. Who knows? Perhaps you'll love it so much, you'll dream up reasons to go hang out in your laundry room. It could happen.

Guiding lights. Like so many rooms, let's start with lighting. In the laundry room, all three types of lighting are vital:

General lighting will get you in the door—no one wants to do laundry in a dark space. We're talking a sunny window and/or a ceiling light with personality and power. Many a bare-bones laundry room has just a single light bulb and a string pull. More than a few scary movies feature just such a room. If that's what you've got, it's time for an immediate upgrade. For starters (and a very small investment), you can add a clip-on ceiling-light cover to that bulb. They're available in numerous sizes, colors, and styles, including fabric drum shades, woven rattan designs, and even faux crystal covers. And they literally attach to that single light bulb in two seconds; thanks to a basic wire frame, no tools are needed.

And don't neglect that light pull—you deserve so much more than a knot at the end of a string. Hundreds of options exist, including brass, glass, leather, pewter, pottery, and wooden pulls in every possible shape and design. Since it's the laundry room, you might even use a clothespin.

To crank up our general-lighting lumens, however, consider replacing that single bulb with a new, more powerful ceiling light. Any light you'd select for another room in your house can be placed in the laundry room. Yes, even a chandelier. Or what about track lighting with a bevy of bulbs, a flush-mount ceiling light (mounted right below your ceiling), one or more pendant lights, a combination ceiling fan and light, or perhaps a statement light fixture in sync with your laundry room décor, say a Tiffany-inspired glass shade or a rustic farmhouse barn light? Or maybe you love a minimal, industrial approach—then consider one of those four-paneled 120-watt LED bulbs; each of these newfangled bulbs cranks out a whopping 12,000 lumens from a single socket while using 80 percent less energy than a similar wattage incandescent light bulb.

As noted in the kitchen chapter, you can install your new fixture with a conversion kit from a hardware store. If your house was built

HL Tip: A small fan makes a great amenity in the laundry room. It speeds the drying process for those wet clothes hanging on a drying rack. It also keeps the air moving, making the room a whole lot fresher.

before 1985, please hire an electrician to ensure your wiring is up to code and your new light fixture will work safely. If your house is newer and you're handy, watch a YouTube how-to video and be sure to turn off the electricity to that room before attempting. If you're not handy, again, ask a knowledgeable friend for help or hire an electrician.

Task lighting is critical for spotting and removing stains, and for sewing on buttons or mending a tear. A tabletop reading light is great for this purpose. You also might consider adding under-cabinet task lighting for close-up tasks. Whether high-tech, direct-wired modular tracks with puck lights or do-it-yourself, stick-on, battery-operated options, your choice will depend on your preference and your budget. Whatever you select, LED bulbs with a rating near 100 will provide all the light you need.

Accent lighting can literally lighten your mood—and who doesn't want that? A lighted garland, a decorative table lamp, or a small light that attaches to a framed poster or painting are all great options. Accent lighting is only limited by your imagination and your pocketbook. The sky's the limit—consider a trio of star-shaped paper shades, a ball light (in homage to all those wool balls in your dryer), or a neon sign in the shape of a hanger. But even an inexpensive set of fairy lights or globe bulbs strung along the ceiling can make a world of difference in an otherwise straightforward laundry room.

HL Tip: Some people go to the Laundromat every week. Others go once in a while. In either case, I recommend leaving the laundry baskets at home and using zippered canvas tote bags instead. They're easy to carry and hold loads. Plus, unlike laundry baskets, items don't tend to fall out. You can also get your bags monogrammed with words like *Dirty Laundry* for fun or *Dirty Harry* just because.

Trick and treat. Trompe l'oeil, a French phrase that means "to trick the eye," is a fun approach to take in a laundry room. Consider trying one of these three ideas:

1. If you don't have a window but you've got extra wall space, hang a mirror, which can reflect your room's light, make the room appear larger, and serve as a substitute window. You might even add narrow white tape across the glass to mimic the look of windowpanes. Or you could frame a photo or poster of a window as a near-perfect replacement. Really love this idea? You could even swap out that window vista twice a year, displaying a wintry view during the colder months and a summery scene the rest of the year—or vice versa.

2. If you've got a concrete floor, consider painting an elaborate or not-so-elaborate rug. Even a large, painted-on red rectangle can add color and pizzazz to your space. Or introduce a surprise on the floor with a self-adhesive, vinyl graphic, like a 3-D koi pond or garden walkway. Or skip the floor and paint or install a ceiling mural, perhaps a faux tin ceiling, a blue sky, or a snowy forest.

3. Applying peel-and-stick wallpaper in a white subway tile or brick pattern can instantly transform your drywall. Come to think of it, you have endless wallpaper options in the laundry room. And bonus: Even if you don't own your home, you can simply remove that hot pink floral or geometrical turquoise motif before you move out.

A fine art. Countless laundry rooms feature a sign that says *Laundry Room.* Yours certainly can, but how about a colorful print of party supplies, a poster of a laundry line, or even a framed vintage clothing ad? Or you might hang those frames that let you swap out your children's drawings week after week. Placing those frames in the laundry room just might inspire Bart and Lisa to join you there to help out.

After returning from a trip abroad where she snapped photos of lots of sheep, my friend blew up her favorite as a laundry room poster. She says washing her wool sweaters at home inspired her. Whatever art you choose, make it something that will lighten your mood every time you step in the room.

Function over form. Remember, this is a working room, so consider how adding a few new features to your laundry space might make your chores easier:

- If you've got a dedicated laundry sink, you might replace a standard faucet with a pullout head, which is great for filling buckets and helping to remove stains. Thankfully, this is an easy do-it-yourself job that should only take an hour to complete.

- Adding a drying rack to your space saves electricity every time you choose it over your dryer. While a wall-mounted accordion rack or swing-out-arm rack saves square footage, a freestanding model provides more rods and, thus, more space for hanging wet clothes. (If your laundry space is tiny or nonexistent, you can always hang wet clothes to dry over a plastic or metal chair in your bathtub.)

- A wall-mounted ironing board also saves space. Some are stowed away behind cabinetry, while others simply flip down. Mine, outfitted in a good-looking black-and-white cover, is always on display, thanks to my ironing board bracket.

- If you've got bare walls and no storage, consider adding a few cupboards or open shelves; then stash supplies in clear glass containers or natural woven baskets (e.g., bamboo, straw, or water hyacinth)—all attractive, environmentally friendly choices.

- Finally, if you've got the space, a small table works great as a place for folding clothes and removing stains. No room? Simply set a piece of plywood, Formica, or what have you across your side-by-side washer and dryer for an instant folding table.

Sink or swim. If your laundry space has no sink, think outside the basin. To handwash delicates, you could buy an extra stainless-steel bowl, like the one you use to make chocolate chip cookies or banana bread. Or you could employ a little galvanized tub that fits inside a cupboard and in which you can store all your laundry supplies. Or here's my fanciest idea: How elegant would laundry day be if you hand-washed your lingerie in Grandma's ruby cut-glass punch bowl? You could even use one of her footed punch cups to pour in the laundry soap. After all, that punch bowl is stored away and you never do seem to make punch. Wait, you do make punch? Then buy another punch bowl dedicated to handwashing. For a great one at a low price, check out a tag sale. (And, Mom, thanks in advance for sending your punch bowl to me—my fingers are crossed every time I go check the mail!)

Contain yourself. Similar to the kitchen, the laundry room is the perfect place to display your everyday tools and supplies. After all, you need them within reach. Dozens of storage solutions exist, but I prefer transparent and/or open options. For example, clear glass containers like vintage candy and canning jars are not only fun to use but also show off exactly which supplies are inside, such as laundry flakes, oxygen bleach, mesh bags, wool balls, safety pins, and more. Or you might rely on matching (and perhaps labeled) fabric or bamboo baskets sans lids so you can quickly grab exactly what you need. Other ideas include antique metal canisters, decorative boxes, and canvas totes. My latest

HL Tip: To keep your washing machine smelling clean, keep the door open after a load finishes to allow drying out. Do the opposite with the dryer and always keep that door closed—during cycles and when not in use. This is a safety issue, especially if you have kids and/or pets.

laundry room addition is a mint julep cup that displays my horsehair brushes. (Now my laundry will always get a blue ribbon!)

Mind the storage. If you're lucky enough to have a few cabinets in your laundry room, you're giving yourself even more cupboard space for every item you place on display. Then, inside those cupboards, you can tuck away extra laundry supplies, household products like garbage bags and microfiber cloths, art and hobby materials, or pet supplies. Or consider relocating your kitchen pantry here. Meanwhile, if those cupboards date back to the 1970s, it might be time to give them a facelift with a fresh coat of paint, removable wallpaper, or more sophisticated knobs.

Basket case. A set of three (or two sets of three) rolling canvas bins is a helpful way to sort your textiles and ensure they're ready to wash. To keep your laundry extra organized, assign and label one laundry basket per bedroom—it'll be obvious whose clothes belong to whom. And if a basket lacks handles, just use a tote bag to bring those dirty clothes to the laundry room.

Going old school. Vintage laundry supplies are crazy fun, and so many options exist, including old laundry signs, vintage magazine ads you can frame, decades-old laundry powder boxes, clamp clothespins, and nonelectric irons. Someday when I have a dedicated laundry room, I'll hang three antique washboards—one each from Granny Dude, Granny Martha, and Ross's mom, Marion; plus my own toy washer will get a place of honor. (By the way, those washboards not only look cool—they really work.)

Matchy, matchy. With clothes, I love mixing things up. But with hangers, I go for matching every time, for both their visual harmony and their performance. In the laundry room, tubular plastic hangers allow you to hang wet clothes to dry. Or, if they're marked for use with wet garments, velvet hangers are phenomenal for drying clothes, and the clothes never fall off!

Make a week of it. If you get all your laundry done in a single day each week, then you can use your laundry room for another purpose

HL Tip: Rather than running up to the kitchen or bathroom for that trusty bottle of 50/50 vinegar-water solution, keep one on hand in the laundry room. In fact, doubling or tripling up on a set of cleaners and tools in the laundry room will save you time and ensure you've got just the cleaner you need, right when you need it. Plus, you won't be tempted to use a cleaner not designated for the right purpose, which means you'll be getting better results. Life is just easier when you're prepared. Also, you might want to keep a vacuum cleaner in the laundry room. Having to haul a vacuum to another floor is both hard on your back and dangerous on stairs.

the other six days. Mine, of course, is a bathroom. But if yours is a dedicated laundry room, you can add a second and maybe even a third purpose:

- Perhaps you love flowers, so you install a small cutting counter plus you tuck clippers, flower wire, and vases into a flower bucket or two under the sink. Let the flower arranging begin.
- Maybe you're a yogi and your furniture-packed living room isn't really conducive to sun salutations. So you add a yoga mat, a candle, a bolster, and a blanket to your laundry room, and suddenly you've got a fitness studio. Namaste.
- Or perhaps your favorite hobby is painting and your laundry room window invites you to pick up your paintbrushes a few times a week.

What new purpose will draw you to your laundry room?

Time to Clean Up

Earlier I said that hanging a disco ball in the laundry room is a must. In fact, the disco ball in my laundry room–bathroom is famous. It's been featured on my TV show, in my laundry videos, and in numerous magazine and newspaper articles. Plus, the fact that it, like nearly every disco ball in the United States, was made in Kentucky (my home state) makes it all the better.

But my suggestion that you hang a disco ball in your laundry room is serious. Life can be hard. Throw in all of the daily demands that are placed on us and our loved ones, and life can become downright overwhelming. Hanging a disco ball plays the foil to all that; this mood-lifting, glittery sphere brings the party to the hardest-working room in your house. And it's difficult not to smile every time you walk in. If you haven't already added a mirror ball to your laundry room, I highly recommend you do. Now let's get cleaning:

- Gather up any items that don't belong in the laundry room and return them; plus, retrieve the laundry room hangers and wool balls that somehow always end up in other rooms of the house.
- Next, wipe away any cobwebs from the ceiling and window(s) with a wool duster. Now turn off the lights and brush off fixtures, including cloth shades, with a horsehair brush. Replace any burnt-out bulbs. And, of course, dust that disco ball.
- Move everything from the sink ledge to the top of the washer and wipe down the sink with a microfiber cloth to which you've added dish soap and water. If the sink needs more scrubbing, sprinkle Bar Keepers Friend (baking soda works in a pinch) and then scrub away with a coir or Tampico brush. Now move back those sink items. They too may need a quick rinse and wipe down. The same may be true of your horsehair brushes, soap dish, and other laundry supplies.

- Next, spray the top of your washing machine and your dryer, plus the gaskets, with the 50/50 vinegar-water solution, and wipe with a microfiber cloth or a clean rag. Next, wipe dry with a clean towel. (It's the laundry room, so you know there's one nearby.) Once a month or so, use a microfiber cloth or microfiber mop to wipe down the walls. And once or twice a year, wipe down any cabinet fronts and interiors as well.

- Also, once or twice a year, when your washing machine is starting to smell, simply pour 1 pound of Borax and 1 gallon of white vinegar directly into your empty washing machine. Then select your hottest, longest cycle. When the cycle is done, your machine will be perfectly clean. And while the washer is running, grab a towel, spray it with the vinegar solution, and wipe the inside of the dryer too.

- Now pick up any clothes off the floor and place them in your sorting bins or laundry baskets. Then roll up any laundry room rugs and shake them out in a garbage can or outside. Throw the rugs in the washer, but don't turn it on yet.

- Next, sweep the floor with a broom or vacuum. If the floor could use more than a quick sweep and you've got a steam cleaner, use it to disinfect, sanitize, and clean. After all, laundry room floors tend to be super linty, and some splotches of cleaning products have likely dripped there as well.

- Inspect your laundry baskets and laundry bags. If needed, wipe down the baskets and throw the bags into the washer too. Then add any dirty cleaning cloths to the washer and run the wash cycle.

- Now's a great time to restock any supplies, including your vinegar solution, the cleaning vodka in your spray bottle, and any laundry room treats. (I won't tell.)

- Come to think of it, finishing cleaning the laundry room calls for a sweet. While you enjoy it, fire up the disco ball and crank some tunes.

The Ten-Minute Clean: Laundry Room

Your new boyfriend is coming over and he's a bit uncoordinated. To avoid any embarrassment if he spills that Neapolitan ice cream down the front of his shirt, you've got to improve the state of your laundry room. He's a gentleman, after all, and you know he'll insist on washing it himself. No worries—even if he arrives in ten minutes, you'll be ready. On second thought, maybe you'll turn on the disco ball, crank the tunes, and purposely spill on him.

- Gather up any items that don't belong in the laundry room and set them aside for returning later.
- Dust the ceiling light, window, and disco ball with a wool duster.
- Wipe down the exterior of the washer and dryer with a clean cloth and the 50/50 vinegar-water solution.
- Pick up any clothes from the floor and throw them in your sorting bins.
- Shake out the rug in the garbage, dust or vacuum the floor if needed, and return the rug to the floor.
- Finally, drip a few drops of essential oil on your wool balls and place them on the counter so your laundry room smells amazing.
- Done! Now's the perfect time to change out of your cleaning clothes. Just throw them in the hamper or wash. (I promise I won't tell anyone if you run through the house in your skivvies!)

My Ten-Minute Cleaning Playlist: Laundry Room (Upbeat)
- "Sir Duke" by Stevie Wonder (3:53)
- "Music for a Sushi Restaurant" by Harry Styles (3:13)
- "Hot Stuff" by Donna Summer (2:55)

My Ten-Minute Cleaning Playlist: Laundry Room (Mellow)
- "FM" by Steely Dan (5:06)
- "Washing Machine Heart" by Mitski (2:08)
- "Style" by Taylor Swift (3:51)

HL Tip: If you have yet to revamp your laundry life, here's a list of items to get started (you likely own many already):

- soap flakes or a high-quality, plant-based liquid laundry soap
- oxygen bleach (100 percent sodium percarbonate)
- washing soda (100 percent sodium carbonate)
- a small horsehair laundry brush and a laundry soap bar
- a spray bottle filled with the 50/50 vinegar-water solution
- a bottle of oil-soap stain solution
- a small bottle of Amodex (a nontoxic ink remover)
- a small spray bottle filled with vodka to remove odors from fabrics
- laundry mesh bags
- safety pins
- a bottle or two of essential oil
- dye-trapping laundry sheets
- several wool balls
- a tube of tennis balls—the balls are great in the dryer with down items
- Oh, and my first book, *Laundry Love: Finding Joy in a Common Chore*

CHAPTER 8

OUTDOOR SPACES
GO OUTSIDE AND PLAY

Frog said, "I wrote 'Dear Toad, I am glad that you are my best friend. Your best friend, Frog.'"
"Oh," said Toad, "that makes a very good letter."
Then Frog and Toad went out onto the front porch to wait for the mail. They sat there, feeling happy together.

—Arnold Lobel, *Frog and Toad Are Friends*

It's only right that I'm enjoying my deck while working on this chapter—especially on a beautiful September day that's one of the first to offer cooling midday breezes. Butterflies bob nearby, two shy rabbits nibble on leaves down below, and cars hum steadily along the street adjacent to our brownstone.

It's a small slice of heaven on my tiny, tree house–like deck, perched off our third floor and filled with plants. This year's virtual jungle includes hot pink Dipladenia (also known as rocktrumpet), every color of coleus you can imagine bursting from my window boxes, white impatiens that glow at night, a plethora of ferns, a type of euphorbia that looks like baby's breath, and spring pansies in orange. I often buy black pansies too—I love their drama—but this year I couldn't find any at my local nursery. Usually, I nurse them both along until Halloween and, truth be told, I buy extra pansies in the fall. And then, of course, there's my lime tree (aka Brian Jones) and my Australian tree fern (which I've yet to name), both of which live outside during the warmer months and take up residence in my bathroom and bedroom respectively the rest of the year. Filling my deck with flowers and plants gives me joy.

Meanwhile, our brown wrought-iron furniture blends right in with the tree house theme. Plus, because the mesh seats don't require cushions, I never have to run outside to grab pillows before a rainstorm hits.

Small as it is, I'm grateful for my deck, which invites me outside year-round, even during winter. I wrap up in a blanket or two to enjoy New Year's Eve fireworks or just to watch snowflakes fall on my window boxes, filled then with spruce tips and fairy lights.

How about you? Does your home's outdoor space invite your presence?

Getting Inspired

Ever since time began, our early hominid ancestors wanted to live indoors. You can't blame them, what with the giant sloths (I love sloths but prefer the smaller ones), woolly mammoths, and saber-toothed cats prowling around. Oh, and the falling meteorites—let's not forget those. In fact, you can draw a through line that begins with caves and ends with four walls and a roof.

Folks wanted to live indoors, at least, until they realized just how nice it is to pair a cold glass of rosé with a new novel on a sunny summer afternoon. That's likely when hammocks and patios were invented. For a good long time now, people have enjoyed the great outdoors.

In this chapter, we focus on the outside spaces at our homes—wherever we enter and exit, where we spend time with family and friends, and where we rest and recharge. Your home might have one, two, or several of these, including:

- **Portico:** This small, covered entryway extends back to the ancient Greeks and provides a grander entrance and exit every time you walk through the door. Many feature columns and some are enclosed by glass on three sides.
- **Porch:** This covered living space often stretches across the front of a house but can wrap around two, three, or, in some generous versions, all four sides. Typical furnishings include rocking chairs, porch swings, and anything made of wicker. And some are fully screened in.
- **Patio:** This uncovered, typically suburban backyard space is built at ground level of tiles, bricks, and/or concrete, and likely features a grill, a picnic table, and a pool (at least the kiddie kind).
- **Lanai:** Speaking of pools, a lanai—à la *The Golden Girls* ("Excuse me, Krystle Carrington!")—often includes a pool and functions like an outdoor living room, with a roof plus screens to accom-

modate outdoor living without the nuisance of bugs and direct
sunlight.

- **Pergola:** This open rooflike structure is supported by posts and
often used on patios for a bit of shade and privacy. Plus, it looks
great with fairy lights, wisteria, and a hanging basket or two. (I
have a bit of pergola envy.)
- **Deck:** This backyard amenity is generally built of lumber and
hangs off the side of a house, although not always. Dressed up for a
cocktail party or down for a barbecue, this space wears well every
day of the week. (Consider it a home's little black dress [LBD].)

When I was growing up, we had a large deck. Stained perhaps un-
surprisingly in black (see LBD reference above), it boasted built-in
seating plus wrought-iron furniture in yellow (Mom's favorite color)
set off by floral cushions. I particularly remember Fourth of July parties when my parents would invite everyone to our breakfast room
with a table laden with every kind of picnic food imaginable. Then
they'd throw open the French doors leading onto the deck. We'd wan-
der back and forth between the indoors and the outdoors, and it truly
felt like a party.

I also recall sitting with my grandparents on their screened back
porch. Granny Dude loved to drink iced tea there, while Granddad
would smoke his pipe. I'd often hang out with them in the evenings,
sometimes digging in to the world's greatest strawberry shortcake, enjoying the cool breezes, or watching fireflies flicker in the surrounding
woods.

But it is my neighbor Ruby's deck that continues to inspire me.
When I was growing up, she had—hands down—the most incredible
patio I'd ever seen. You entered through a sliding glass door where
an overhang protected the grill and a built-in bench offered a place
for the cook to bide her time while the steaks sizzled—it was an outdoor kitchen before that was even a thing. The floor was a stylish black
slate—and the inspiration for my own slate bathroom floor. A stone

ledge encircled the patio and a teak storage box kept her French bistro chairs at the ready for a party. Finally, all along the back of the patio was an arbor where grapes grew. Just imagine reaching up for a handful while you relaxed on the glider underneath!

How would you like someone to describe your patio, deck, or lanai?

Time to Freshen Up

For decades, designers and home builders have been creating outdoor living rooms, outfitting them with couches and club chairs, stone or brick fireplaces, flat-screen TVs, hot tubs, pool houses, and more. But your home doesn't need to achieve *Architectural Digest* status for you to enjoy the great outdoors. You simply need some ingenuity and imagination, and to pay attention to your senses—seeing, hearing, tasting, smelling, and touching. If your outdoor space attends to all the senses, you'll have created a place that's hard to resist—for example:

- seeing your favorite tree or flowering bushes
- listening to crickets, spring peepers ("chorus frogs"), and a bubbling fountain
- tasting tomatoes and strawberries right off the vine
- smelling those lovely lilacs in the spring or that smoky bonfire in the fall
- resting your head on a cushy pillow on your hammock or touching the leaves of soft plants like lamb's ear

Last summer, everyone on our block of fourteen 1880s brownstones got new decks, all built by Carlos, John, and their expert team. To say our neighborhood was thrilled is an understatement. While we brought these hard workers food and drink, they kept the mood fun and light, despite the construction, with great music playing. In just a month, they transformed not only our decks but also our neighborhood. Suddenly, we were all spending time outside and getting to know one another better than ever before.

As a thanks for our hospitality, the construction team generously gifted each brownstone four window boxes. Before this, while our plants lived on our deck, Ross and I rarely did. Now we're out there daily, enjoying the space, our plants, and our new furniture.

Where are you on the scale of outdoor enjoyment at home? Do you practically live outside when the weather is nice? Or perhaps you enjoy dinner on the patio a few days a week? Maybe you like to welcome the day on the front porch with coffee and the newspaper, or maybe your schedule is so busy that you forget to visit your outdoor spaces at all. Suddenly the weather isn't so accommodating and, once again, you're waiting until next year to truly appreciate them. Wherever you find yourself, let's increase the amount and quality of your outdoor living with a verdant variety of ideas.

Door to door. Whether it's the front door, which happens to be on your front porch, or the back door, which opens into the garage, or perhaps a side door, which opens onto a patio, every door makes a statement about your home. Ensuring each door's look is put together not only boosts your home's appeal, curb and otherwise, but it also makes you happy every time you enter.

HL Tip: Similar to revamping your door, you can transform your mailbox in a flash with a can of spray paint. A personalized address decal in a modern font adds a thoughtful touch too. Or switch out your mailbox entirely. Dozens of styles exist, enabling you to match your mailbox to your home's architecture—say, a traditional mailbox for a saltbox house or a minimalist mailbox for a midcentury modern home. However you enhance your mailbox, checking for the mail will be all the more enjoyable— even when it hasn't been delivered yet.

One of the easiest ways to transform a door is with paint. This relatively small canvas can be transformed on a sunny morning with a paint roller, angle brush, primer, and paint (based on your type of door—wood, metal or fiberglass) in whatever hue that makes your heart sing. Think of it like the perfect throw pillow on that expanse of couch. Want a new look? Simply paint again.

My front door is a vivid orange, and since we live in one of fourteen identical limestone brownstones, it's nice to be able to tell the pizza place to deliver to the one with the orange door. (If you've got a portico over your front door or a front porch ceiling, you may want to consider painting it haint blue. Even if you must abide by the rules of a homeowners' association, that ceiling can't be seen from the street, so you're good to go. For more on haint blue, turn to page 100.)

Here are two more thoughts on quickly transforming the overall look of your door:

First, as a kid, I remember many neighbors covering their front doors with Christmas wrapping paper to mimic the look of a present. Some even attached gigantic ribbon bows. But who says you have to wait for the holidays? You can wrap your front door for any old reason—your mood, a new season, or a special occasion, like a birthday party or graduation celebration.

Second, I really love it when I walk by a glass door (or a window for that matter) that's been decorated with flowers or leaves with the help of colorful paint pens, especially made for drawing on glass. What a joyful surprise!

How else can you change the look of your door? With bling—in brass, bronze, chrome, nickel, or pewter. Hardware is to a door like jewelry is to an outfit. Consider the doorknob, the door knocker, the kickplate, and the doorbell. Oh, the doorbell! As a kid, I loved Aunt Lucy's Victorian model. It was mechanical—you simply turned the small decorative handle on the outside of the door, and a corresponding bell on the other side of the door rang. I loved that doorbell so much that my parents eventually installed one on our front door.

Whatever your taste or home's architectural style, you'll find loads of hardware options at brick-and-mortar and online hardware stores. And don't hesitate to look for one-of-a-kind vintage options at flea markets, yard sales, and antique stores.

Lastly, don't forget the accessories that really make a door, and your home, welcoming. They might include a chair, potted plants like topiaries, a floor lantern or two, a fancy floor mat, and/or a wreath.

Wreaths are traditionally hung on front doors during the holidays, but you can use these decorative rings year-round. Wonderful live options include those made of flowers, bay leaves, magnolia leaves, eucalyptus, succulents, and fruits like lemons and apples.

Just as beautiful are wreaths constructed of dried flowers, silk flowers, herbs like lavender and rosemary, and feathers. For one that's perfect for your front door, you might also consider checking online marketplaces for artist-created options made of surprising materials, such as burlap, felt, steel, and even recycled nautical rope. Want something other than a wreath? You could hang a handled Nantucket basket, traditionally hung on a door and used for mail; a plaque that features your family name; or a removable decal that reads *Welcome* or *Hello!*

A light touch. I wasn't thrilled when a narrow pipe was installed to encase the wires leading from my house to my deck light. But then I bought eight-foot-long curly willow branches and lashed them on with florist wire, disguising the pipe and adding beauty to the space. Now I've noticed a neighbor has done the same. As I keep discovering, outdoor lighting calls for creativity.

Consider the light by your front door. Does its color, shape, size, and style make sense for your house? Sometimes we inherit an exterior light or lights that used to work for the previous homeowners, but since moving in, the front porch or maybe the whole house has been revamped. Suddenly, the exterior lighting no longer works in any number of ways.

Fortunately, outdoor lights come in every style—including traditional, farmhouse, craftsman, transitional, contemporary, and industrial. Finishes vary too, including brushed, matte, and polished. What type of glass do you like—clear, frosted, or seeded? How about your bulbs—Edison, incandescent, LED? With all of these options, you might start to worry over price, but replacing a light on a front porch can cost as much as five thousand dollars for an antique reproduction of an elaborate hanging lantern or as little as ten bucks for an old-fashioned yet stylish Edison bulb. Obviously you can find lights to fit your budget.

Once you're happy with your general lighting, i.e., pendant and sconce lights, you can jazz up your outdoor space with task lighting (say, for pouring margaritas) and decorative lighting. Options for the former include lanterns, table lamps, and floor lamps. Some examples of the latter include the obvious: individual strings of fairy or bulb lights. But many others exist, including curtains of string lights, glowing tabletop orbs, colorful solar lights in shapes like butterflies and flowers, wired or solar pathway lights, and so many more.

If you haven't used rope lights before, they're a perfect outdoor choice. These simple string lights, encased in plastic tubes, connect end to end up to 300 feet. They're also super malleable, so they can be draped in a tree, wrapped around a deck railing, tucked along the edge of a garden, run along a pathway or an overhang, or even shaped into a word or two, like *Happy* or *Love*, on an outdoor wall. (Just resist using *Live, Laugh, Love*.)

Even if your outdoor space is tiny, don't let that stop you from hanging lights. For example, place a bamboo pole into a metal can to which you've added quick-drying cement. Make several, set them around your space, and then string lights from one to another. Best of all, these mobile pots can be stored when not in use and set up in a new configuration when used again.

Turn over a new leaf. A while back, I visited New York City often and always walked the same route. One brownstone I'd pass by regularly featured an oversized window box filled with ivy and three pots of pansies. Of course I noticed, because I love pansies. In the summer, the ivy was still there, but the pansies had been swapped for red geraniums. And in the fall, three pumpkins were featured, right along with the ivy. I thought the owners' approach to their window box was brilliant—and so easy.

Growing plants doesn't have to be hard. Or intimidating. If you're just getting started or if your space is small, all you need is a plant or two from your local nursery or even the grocery store. Bring them home, plunk them in pots, and suddenly you've added life and greenery and color to your outdoor space. I place all my plants in papier-mâché liners and then put those in my ceramic and resin pots. That way, when I'm switching out my summer geraniums for fall mums or ornamental cabbage, I simply lift them out and don't need to wash out the pots. Composting is easier too.

If you love to cook, consider adding herbs to your plant party. Or if you entertain outside or plan to start, select two or three white flowering plants for your patio or deck and group them together for a mini moon garden, so called because silvery and white plants and flowers glow in the moonlight.

HL Tip: Overwhelmed by floral choices at a plant nursery? Use these three tricks to make your selections easier and elevate your home's curb appeal:

1. Choose flora to match your front door. For example, perhaps your front door is yellow. Then grow yellow flowers, such as daffodils, marigolds, or sunflowers.
2. Select flowers that complement your door. Working with that same yellow door, these could be blue blooms, like delphinium, salvia, or lobelia.
3. Or establish a color palette. Once again, a yellow door would suggest yellow, blue, and white flowers, so they'd all coordinate and complement one another.

Like to branch out from small plants? Consider investing in a tree or two. We all know that trees improve our air, provide shade, offer food and protection for birds, and much more. If you've got a yard, you're golden. But if you don't have a yard, you could plant a slow-growing ornamental tree in a resin container (porcelain pots can break in freezing temperatures).

Even in the frigid north, you can enjoy a container tree year-round. First, you need to know your planting zone. If you're not in the know, a planting zone (there are now thirteen) is a geographic area determined by its average minimum temperature—key to a plant's survival. Simply subtract two planting zones when you're selecting your tree. For example, Minnesota falls in USDA Zone 4, so I choose trees that thrive in Zone 2 like a dwarf Alberta spruce, a miniature cone-shaped tree, or a hardy Amur chokecherry, known for its flowers and edible blackberries. What zone are you in and what trees could thrive on your patio or deck? Experts at a local garden center or nursery can help you find those answers.

Another benefit of a container tree is that you can even enjoy it from inside your home, watching it through the window when you wake up in the morning or noticing its fairy lights twinkling just before you crawl into bed.

Faux flower power. Not all of us have green thumbs. And some of us with green thumbs might be pluck out of time to nurture, fertilize, or even water our plants. Either way, faux flowers and plants are so good these days that even Miss Marple (or should I say Miss Maple?) might not be able to tell the difference.

Every summer a friend of mine pulls a fake cherry tomato plant out of storage. It's in a seemingly weathered flowerpot, but just like those bright red and soft green tomatoes, even the weathering is artificial. This imitation veg plant looks so real that guests have been known to pluck a tomato right off the plant only to be stopped just before popping that little red orb into their mouths. No lie.

Beyond ersatz veggies, you can find fake ivies and bougainvilleas to tuck into pottery wall pockets, potted cacti and Boston ferns, hanging geraniums and philodendrons, glorious silk orchids and palms, ficus and pine trees, boxwood topiaries, and so much more. Best of all, these marvelous plants never require water or sun. Just dust them once a month with a feather duster.

Splish, splash. You may have heard that listening to recorded water gurgling—via a phone or white noise machine—can help you rest and even fall asleep. But what if you could listen to the real thing while lying in your hammock or dining on your patio? (For those of you who live on a lake, river, or ocean, you might want to skip this section; and, yes, I'm jealous.) If you haven't already added a water fountain to your outdoor spaces, rest assured you'll find lots of options to love—including porcelain, stone, and copper; tall or squat; simple or multilevel; plug-in or solar powered. You can even find fountains with built-in planters and LED lights for nighttime entertaining; others are hydroponic, supporting plant life without soil (water lilies, anyone?), and aquaponic, supporting both fish and plants.

Styles are wide-ranging as well, including contemporary (such as boxy concrete designs), down-home (like those created from a whisky or wine barrel), whimsical (a pelican- or frog-themed design, for example), and even magical (like a pitcher that seemingly pours an unending supply of water into an oversized bowl).

Best of all, you can create your own fountain in minutes with just two items: a ceramic planter and an electric pump from the hardware store. Simply fill the planter with water, place the pump inside, and flip the switch—so easy! Even simpler? Drop a solar-powered pump into your ceramic bowl filled with water. Then place it in direct sunlight and soon the water will begin circulating. Or place it in your birdbath—imagine the cute videos you could take of birds splashing in their own fountain!

Feather your nest. Speaking of birdbaths, perhaps all the entertainment you need is fluttering nearby—if certain features are added to your yard. Fresh water allows birds to drink and bathe, and a bubbling fountain, as suggested earlier, is especially attractive to them. Of course, our feathered friends have to eat too, so adding one or more bird feeders is a good idea; you can even attract particular types of birds based on the feeders themselves—for example, a covered ground feeder for cardinals and juncos, or an easy-to-clean glass liquid feeder for hummingbirds. Plants and shrubs should offer nearby protection. And a birdhouse is a good addition as well. A friend of mine has had her three-story, ten-hole virtual bird hotel for twenty years. It's filled with young sparrow families. And hanging right nearby is a small wire basket of her dogs' trimmed fur, a popular choice for weaving into their nests.

Make sparks fly. Around the world, people are drawn to fire like moths to a, well, you know. As we spend more and more time at our homes, friends and neighbors are gathering with us around backyard fires. In fact, since buying a firepit, Ross and I have started inviting people over many weekends.

In the United States, you can find every possible backyard iteration of a fire-producing construct, including Japanese hibachis, Mexican gourd-shaped chiminea, in-ground grills, and even traditional brick fireplaces with built-in pizza ovens. Meanwhile, dozens of firepits exist, in all sizes and price points, including wood-burning and gas-fired. Handheld tins invite you to light teeny-tiny bonfires to enjoy for up to five hours; you can even roast marshmallows with them! And let's not forget those outdoor tables of steel, iron, aluminum, and concrete that feature dramatic gas-fired bonfire centers. Whatever your budget, there's a fire option available for you and your crowd. If you're handy, you might consider building your own—plenty of plans exist for relatively affordable and easy-to-build fireplaces.

Let it glow. If you like a quieter light, candles are always a good idea, especially when tucked into containers that block breezes. Of course you can purchase lanterns, which work well. But so do canning jars, jam jars, and flowerpots—just slip a votive in each. Or you

HL Tip: For inexpensive yet charming party lighting, gather up six or more canning jars. Wrap each jar neck three times with floral wire and then create a loop to hang the jar with another piece of floral wire synched around the neck wire. Drop a votive candle, wax or battery operated, in each, and hang them from a tree or a stretch of twine hung from your pergola. As easy as they are to make, they're simply magical at night.

HL Tip: Is your outdoor space postage stamp–sized? You can still enjoy it. Just introduce to the space these five items: a collapsible café table, two folding chairs, one potted plant, and a chunky candle. Now the stage is set for rest and relaxation.

might place a bunch of tall cathedral candles inside a deep planter for a bigger glow without the major flames. Spraying metallic paint inside the jars, flowerpots, or planters and then letting the paint dry before adding the candles increases the radiance and is a nice juxtaposition with such simple containers. And no, you don't need to use citronella candles, unless you like that lemony scent. Citronella doesn't ward off mosquitoes any more than smoke from other types of candles. (A better bet? Turn on a fan outside—mosquitoes struggle to fly near fans. My fan uses a battery from my tool system.)

In the winter, one of my favorite ways to enjoy candles outside combines balloons and water (temperatures must be below 32°F). Before a party, I fill balloons roughly three-quarters of the way with water and place them outside, along a pathway to my front door. Make sure not to overfill them or you'll just have a pointy shape and no place to nestle a candle. Be sure to set the balloons upside down, on the fattest part of the balloons with the tie at the top. Shortly before the party, cut off the tie and the balloon should slide right off. Then place a votive into the top of each icy balloon shape. Elegant and easy! (You can also buy luminary ice molds—I bought one for Ross years ago and he still likes to make them.)

A banner day. A bright burst of colors, thanks to a banner, bunting, flag, or spinning wind sock can bring smiles to the faces of passersby. Adding one to your front porch, back entrance, or both can instantly lift your own mood too every time you drive up or walk in the door. Other options include a Mexican banner in party colors, a bunting in hues that complement your outdoor décor, or a banner that features a custom message, such as *Summertime*. I have one banner that reads *Please Leave by 9*. Truthfully, no one ever leaves by 9 P.M., but I think it's funny so I always hang it up at parties.

My favorite banners are designed by David Ti, a world-renowned fabric artist who creates complex graphics inspired by Native American designs in rainbow palettes. Arrestingly kaleidoscopic, they can hang outside throughout most of the year, thanks to their heavy-duty, UV-resistant fabric. Only during frigid winter temperatures do they need to be brought inside.

Art of the possible. Twenty years or so ago, Minnesota sculptor Barb Ryan's annual show would open every year on Mother's Day. Her whimsical and humorous giant clay masks (e.g., a frog, a puffin, and a unicorn) were displayed at a plant nursery, each one hanging on a tree. Within days, they'd have all sold and the new owners were just as likely to hang them on their own trees as they were to add them to their walls. That story is a nice reminder that art, at least weather-resistant art, can live outdoors. Think of sculpture gardens. Myriad glass, metal, and concrete artworks are constantly featured outside.

But you don't have to be as fancy as all that. You might consider creating a gallery wall on your back patio with themed images (such as a bunch of suns) cut out of magazines or scrounged up at garage sales. Or you could hang a vintage window off the side of your front porch, add a mirror to reflect various plantings in a corner of your garden, or even attach an interestingly shaped branch to a wall.

Found objects make great additions as well—consider placing an old screen door at the entryway to your garden, planting flowers in the basket of a vintage bike, creating an edge to your garden with upside-down wine bottles (so much prettier than plastic edging and earth-friendly too), hanging a wire chandelier from a tree, adding googly eyes to a spot on your fence, displaying small potted plants on an old ladder, featuring vintage farm implements in your garden, or hanging a garden gate or delicate section of wrought-iron fencing on the wall.

Time to Clean Up

A wonderful book, *Last Child in the Woods* by Richard Louv, touts the importance of spending time in nature for physical and emotional health. I wholeheartedly agree. But not all of us can regularly explore the Appalachian Trail, the Boundary Waters, or even a local park. Instead, a front porch, backyard, or fire escape will do nicely, thank you very much. Spending time outside reduces stress, recharges mental energy, improves sleep, and so much more. That's all the more reason to clean our outdoor spaces so we can truly enjoy them.

- Begin with your corn broom, wiping away any cobwebs from the ceiling and any windows.
- Now turn off the lights and gently brush off the light fixtures with a horsehair brush. Replace any burnt-out bulbs.
- Gather up any items that don't belong in your outside space (e.g., plates, glasses, and bottles) and return them to the kitchen.
- On your way back outside, spray the glass door and any windows with your 50/50 vinegar-water solution and wipe dry. Now polish the doorknob with a clean rag or microfiber cloth.

- If you're at the front of your house, spray the mailbox with the vinegar solution and wipe dry.
- Sweep away leaves and flower petals from the floor of your outdoor space. Or use a small, cordless shop blower to blow them away. You can also use the blower to direct the leaves and grass away from your sidewalk and back into your yard.
- Remove bird "blessings," plus any other stains, from upholstery and any pillows with the vinegar solution and a stiff brush. Outdoor fabrics are sturdy and meant to get wet, so don't worry about scrubbing away. If the covers are removable, feel free to throw them in the wash once or twice a year. Then return them to the cushions or pillows while still damp.
- Wipe down furniture, including glass-topped tables, with a clean rag or microfiber cloth plus the vinegar solution. Once or twice a year, you might also want to pressure-wash the furniture.
- Spray the water fountain and wipe it down. To prevent algae from growing, add 1 cup of vinegar to the water in a small fountain and 2 cups of vinegar to the water in a large fountain. Also, use a rubber band to secure a section of pantyhose—in whatever color matches your fountain—over the pump to prevent leaves from being drawn into the mechanism.
- Wind chimes, planters, and other miscellaneous items could all use a regular cleaning as well. Put that vinegar solution to work.
- If a grill is part of your outdoor space, spray the exterior with the vinegar solution and wipe down. Then soak the grates in a solution of 2 tablespoons oxygen bleach and 1 quart water; let soak for ten minutes or so and scrub with a natural brush. Don't use metal brushes—their bristles can come loose and end up in your food.
- Shake out the doormat and rug. Or place the rug over the rail of the deck and beat with a broom handle to loosen the dirt and sand.
- Lastly, sweep the floor with your corn or deck broom.
- Now refresh your beverage, stretch out on your outdoor couch or hammock, and sing with the birds.

The Ten-Minute Clean: Outdoor Spaces

You completely forgot about St. Urho's Day, and your Finnish American relatives are on their way over for the annual bonfire and feast of squeaky cheese and cloudberry wine. Never mind—you can whip your outdoor space into great shape, or hyvässä kunnossa, in no time. Most important is flipping the switch on that backyard sauna.

- Gather up any items that don't belong in your outside space and return them to the kitchen—or hide them under an upside-down flowerpot.
- Wipe down furniture with a clean rag or microfiber cloth plus the 50/50 vinegar-water solution.
- Sweep away leaves and flower petals from the floor or use a small, cordless shop blower (or hair dryer in a pinch) to blow them away.
- Spray only the area on the glass door with fingerprints, near the doorknob, with the vinegar solution and wipe dry.
- Lastly, freshen up any flowers, light some candles, and prepare to relax.

My Ten-Minute Cleaning Playlist: Outdoor Spaces (Upbeat)
- "You Make Me Feel (Mighty Real)" by Sylvester (6:34)
- "Outside" by George Michael (4:44)

My Ten-Minute Cleaning Playlist: Outdoor Spaces (Mellow)
- "Lovely Day" by Bill Withers (4:15)
- "Hot Fun in the Summertime" by Sly and the Family Stone (2:37)
- "I Will Survive" by Gloria Gaynor (3:18)

HL Tip: For a welcoming glow on a dark porch, loop a string of lights around a wreath. A simple battery pack with a timer will ensure it lights every evening.

SIT A SPELL

Whether your outdoor furniture is built-in, purchased, or a combination of the two, the right furniture can make a huge difference to the function of your outdoor space.

Outdoor furniture falls into four basic categories: wrought iron, resin, wicker, and wood.

As I mentioned before, our wrought-iron furniture with mesh seats serves us perfectly and will for decades to come. Plus, the benefits of wrought iron are numerous—it's heavy, so it's unlikely to move or tip over in strong winds. It comes in an extensive variety of styles, colors, and finishes, so there's bound to be an option you love. And, while more expensive than resin or wicker, it gives you more bang for your buck, being the strongest, most durable, and longest lasting of the options. The cherry on top? It's super easy to clean with soap and water.

Its only downsides are its tendency to heat up on hot days and to rust when exposed to lots of moisture, so it requires regular maintenance. Similar positive and negative attributes can be found in aluminum and stainless-steel furniture, although aluminum is less expensive and lightweight, while stainless steel rarely rusts and can be an environmentally friendly option if made of recycled steel.

Resin furniture is the least expensive of the various types of outdoor furniture and comes in a variety of styles—you've likely seen sophisticated resin couches and chairs made to look like wicker. Resin is resistant to mold and mildew, and it's lightweight, making rearranging an easy task, even for one person. Being lightweight is also a drawback—don't be surprised if it tips over or moves during a storm. Plus, it doesn't last as long as other options.

Wicker furniture likely brings to mind Grandma's front porch and old-fashioned love seats and side tables woven from bamboo, rattan, seagrass, or willow. But its origins extend much longer ago—five thousand years, in fact—to ancient Egypt. Wicker has endured because of its environmentally friendly materials, its lightweight construction, and its cool vibe. Wicker furniture is often used indoors where the weather has no impact, but it can be placed outside. If it begins to show mold and mildew growth, this can be removed with the 50/50 vinegar-water solution as long as it's treated right away. You can also spray lacquer on wicker furniture once a year to ensure it's water resistant.

Wood furniture, specifically teak, is in a class all its own. Not only is its golden color super appealing in an outdoor setting, but teak—thanks to its natural oils—also resists damage from sun, salty air, moisture, and sand. Plus, it's strong and durable: People who store teak when not in use can expect it to last up to fifty years. Its downside? Cost. It's one of the most expensive options due to high demand and limited availability. And unfortunately due to tropical deforestation, it's less sustainable than other hardwoods used for outdoor furniture, including eucalyptus, tropical Shorea, and white oak. You might also encounter ipe wood furniture; ipe is also less sustainable than other hardwoods and is even more expensive than teak.

Whatever furniture you select, keep in mind your space and the way you use it (e.g., entertaining), your climate, whether you have space for storage, and the amount of work you want to put into maintaining the furniture. Checking all these boxes for your purposes will help ensure your furniture choice is a good one.

CHAPTER 9

GARAGE
THE GREAT BEYOND

A clean basement, garage, and attic
are signs of an empty life.

—Doug Larson

When I proposed hosting a Halloween party for every kid in my third-grade class at Prichard Elementary School, my mom didn't balk. But she also knew that our house couldn't accommodate dozens and dozens of costumed kids revved up on punch and Pop Rocks. So she and a friend transformed our two-car garage into a spooky space filled with 1970s Halloween decorations, including crepe-paper ghosts, jointed skeletons with posable limbs, and tagboard cutouts of black cats silhouetted against orange moons.

Not only did our garage offer plenty of space for all of the mini witches, princesses, and monsters munching on caramel apples and Halloween candy, but also when it became a bit too hot inside, Mom could just open the garage door so we kids could play outside.

To clean up the next morning, she sprayed down the concrete floor with the hose and rinsed away every bit of the black-and-orange party residue.

And I know what you're wondering: I wore a little red devil costume, complete with horns.

A garage is too often viewed as simply a place to park the car or store household goods. But a garage is often the most generously sized space in an entire house and can be used for all kinds of purposes. It also very often operates as the front door, in all but name, for the people who reside in the house. You pull into the garage and access your house via the garage door. It makes sense then, for these myriad purposes and its role as another front door, to keep the garage clean and tidy. The space can be as welcoming and serene as your entryway.

Getting Inspired

Before early automobile owners transformed their carriage houses into garages, these spaces were used for far more than vehicle storage; initially, many still housed livestock. (After a few months, imagine how those car seats smelled!) Today, roughly 65 percent of housing units have a garage or carport, and those spaces serve as band studios, entrepreneurial launching pads, apartments, and more.

I remember a while back seeing a woman's garage featured in a home magazine. She'd painted the walls, added art, and even hung a chandelier. Most of the time, her garage simply stored her vehicle. But whenever she entertained a crowd, she simply backed out her car, set up a dining table, and, abracadabra, her garage was a dining room.

One thing a significant percentage of garages don't do is store cars. In fact, 25 percent of people with two-car garages never park in them, according to a U.S. Department of Energy study. Instead, these rooms are viewed as living and storage spaces. Moreover, nearly 25 percent of respondents to an Impulse Research survey said their plethora of stuff makes them too embarrassed to ever open their garage doors. Fortunately, it's also true that in most cases adopting a new organizational approach can open up a good deal of that precious garage space.

If you have a garage, how do you use it? Is it simply to park your car(s) and for storage? Or maybe it's also your home office, the place you work out, or where you tinker at a workbench? Friends of mine used to have a neighbor whose garage was so rigged out as a workshop that it even featured a urinal so he could avoid tracking wood shavings or paint into his house during bathroom breaks. That makes sense to me, although my friends did say it was odd to see him standing before this workshop WC when they took their Saturday-morning walk.

Time to Freshen Up

However you use your garage today, there are lots of ways to make the most of this valuable space without breaking the bank. What follows are some organizational ideas and revitalizing strategies. Let's get started.

Garage of another color. I'll never understand not painting garage walls. The garage is likely your family's front door, and I know I don't want to drive in, or walk in, to face studs or blah-colored walls. If that's your situation, you can change it up: Remove everything from the garage, mask off the windows and doors with tape and plastic sheets, and cover the floors with drop cloths or rolls of brown floor-protector paper. Then borrow or rent an airless sprayer to paint those walls in just a couple of hours.

Awhile back, my sister-in-law fell in love with the metallic paint Ross and I had used in our kitchen. So she bought enough to make over her garage, and honestly, it looks fantastic. That said, when painting a garage, consider using upcycled paint, which keeps old paint out of landfills; several brands offer this eco-friendly option. For a double-car garage, you'll need around four gallons; for a single-car garage, two or three gallons should do the job.

Take the floor. Historically, the floors of garages have been ignored, typically left as raw concrete. But that's no longer the case. Applying concrete floor paint or epoxy-based paint makes garage floors more reflective and therefore brighter, diminishes the dust that comes from the concrete itself, and makes the floor both easier to clean and more resistant to stains. This affordable project takes just one or two gallons, and the paint comes in lots of colors. Plus, you can paint designs on it. How about a graphic design for a punch of color? Or a racetrack for those rainy days when your kids still need to get some energy

HL Tip: Are you hosting Thanksgiving but worried about having enough space? Turn your garage into a killer staging area. A picnic or folding table can accommodate lots of slow cookers, instant pots, and convection burners—keeping everything hot or warm, while you await the perfect, roasting, all-important turkey. When you're ready to eat, just fill up your serving platters and bowls here, and bring them back inside.

out, perhaps zipping around on trikes and scooters? Or paint the floor in zones to make it clear where the fitness area ends and the car goes. To make the paint last as long as possible, you may want to consider using sealer.

For a garage floor that's polished and posh, consider an epoxy coating, which is easy to clean, resists fading, provides soundproofing, and is customizable in numerous colors, finishes, and designs. Depending on your budget, you can install it yourself or hire a professional service. Produced by refining crude oil, a polluting process, epoxy isn't great for the environment; it generally can't be recycled and isn't biodegradable. That said, this organic compound lasts up to a decade, making it arguably sustainable since you won't need to replace it for years. You can even find recyclable, compostable epoxy resin.

Grab some bench. For as long as I can remember, my mom has kept a potting bench in the garage. This wood bench features a nice counter-height workspace, plus shelves above for pots and tools, and a tub below for potting soil. She uses hers to sow seeds, freshen up and repot houseplants, and create hanging baskets.

While you can purchase a wooden, vinyl, or metal potting bench for north of one or two hundred dollars, a vintage dresser, old shelving unit, or even a sheet of plywood attached to a couple of sawhorses can do the job just fine. Just paint or stain it to your liking, and then stock it with everything you need.

Mind the storage. Perhaps you've got an athletic family who needs to pack away surfing, curling, and badminton gear. Or your outdoorsy family could outfit an entire Scouts troop—well, that camping gear needs storing too. Or maybe you need to stash your gardening gear— shovels, spades, hoes, and rakes. Oh, and don't forget your hobby supplies and your holiday decorations. Where to begin?

Let's start with cabinets. Wall-mounted garage cabinets need not be fancy, although plenty of them are. Think walls of sleek steel customized cabinets in matte or lustrous finishes of any color you desire. Plenty of these flexible cabinet systems can be found at and installed by professional cabinet installers. Your local hardware store may even offer options that you can install yourself.

Perhaps better yet, hang on to your old kitchen cabinets after a remodel and move them into your garage. Or buy used cabinets from a reuse center that specializes in offering home-improvement items leftover from others' projects. Or find old lockers available from online classified ads. Regardless of the source, these options are a great way to hide away whatever needs storing in your garage. Close up those cabinet doors and the space will look practically pristine.

Other storage options are as simple as plastic tubs with tight-fitting lids—you can stack them on the floor or load them onto heavy-duty metal shelving. The only issue with this approach is remembering what's inside. Rather than scrawling the contents across each one with a Sharpie (and then inevitably crossing out what you wrote and relabeling them down the road), I'd recommend using oversized labels from an office-supply store.

Or select a theme you're drawn to—say, album covers. Then print out smaller-scale versions of your favorites, label those with the contents of each box and tape each one on with clear packing tape. Seeing all those album covers when you step into the garage will make you smile. Other themes might include graphic images of places you want to visit someday or cars you've owned or want to purchase in the future. Heck, your garage storage could serve as a huge vision board.

Lighten up. Second to the stereotypical basement, the stereotypical garage wins the award for being dark and dingy. But there's no reason that should be the case. Like any other room in your house, a garage should include natural light and a variety of other light sources. If your garage lacks windows, you could add a picture or casement window or a traditional or tubular skylight.

Beyond natural light, don't hesitate to boost your general and task-lighting lumens. If you want to add decorative lighting, maybe for your fitness area, more power to you—literally. As for general lighting, consider affordable, earth-friendly LED lights, which use at least 75 percent less energy than incandescent lights, last up to 25 times longer, and save you money. Plus, in the garage, they perform well no matter how far the temperature drops, unlike some fluorescent lights.

Additionally, LEDs come in a variety of color temperatures (warm is generally preferred in the garage) and configurations, including flush-mounted ceiling lights and undercabinet lights. For an even easier install without wiring, you can find LEDs as battery-powered puck lights for undercabinet lighting.

Or stock up on affordable clamp lamps available at any hardware store. In my first apartment I used a bevy of them with chrome-topped bulbs for an industrial-chic look. You can use these cheap task lights anywhere, but they're especially effective in the garage. Plug them into a power strip, and with a flick of a switch, you've got all the light you need for that furniture-refinishing project or whatever you're working on.

In the zone. The key to garage organization is creating zones. And those zones will be personal, depending on who's using the garage and how they're using it. Perhaps the fourth of the garage nearest the entrance to your home serves as your office, while your car takes up most of the rest of the space, plus there's a bit of storage. Well, those are three zones. Making sure those zones work for you is important, as is ensuring that everyone who uses the garage understands those zones. As I mentioned before, you can visually separate those zones by painting the floor of those spaces different colors or by setting up room dividers.

Other zones might include a pseudo mudroom outfitted with hooks for coats and a tray for boots and shoes; a fitness area, complete with a treadmill; and a space you use to update old furniture with paint and ingenuity. Again, your zones should fit your needs.

It's likely that a storage zone or multiple storage zones will be part of your plan. As you decide on where to place things, keep items you access most often—like those eighty-five rolls of toilet paper, thirty-six cans of soup, and twelve tubes of hair gel—near your entryway. This way you can just step out and grab what you need without having to walk through the garage. On the other hand, keep the outdoor tools near the large garage door. That way, as you're working in your yard, you can just reach in to return one tool and grab another.

Getaway car. I've always recommended the laundry room as a great place for a little alone time. After all, when you announce you're going to the laundry room to throw another load in, who's going to follow you—or know you're actually hanging out there reading a magazine or listening to your favorite podcast while sipping a glass of wine? (It's also got that great disco ball—which would be a fabulous addition to your garage, come to think of it.)

But once you transform your garage, you'll have another place to hang out: your vehicle. Honestly, back when I was pitching this book, I took my first virtual meeting in my parked car. And since then, I've had multiple phone and online business and medical meetings in my car. It's a great place to work if you need a quiet space away from your sleeping partner, your playful kids, or even your demanding pets. Just don't turn on the car in a closed garage—that's dangerous!

Time to Clean Up

Garages are often the only space in the house that we annually devote a day or even a whole weekend to cleaning up and cleaning out. Follow the steps below for a thoughtful cleanup.

- Begin with a smaller corn broom, wiping away any cobwebs from the ceiling and windows.
- Now turn off the lights (perhaps you'll need to open your large garage door so you can see!) and brush off the light fixtures with a horsehair brush. Replace any burnt-out bulbs.
- Before you break out the 50/50 vinegar-water solution, you may want to apply a shop vacuum to every surface first. Or blow all that dust to the floor before you sweep.

- Garage windows are notoriously dusty and dirty. Clean them with the vinegar solution and a microfiber cloth.
- Wipe down all those dusty cabinets and various storage containers with the vinegar solution and a microfiber cloth.
- If you've got any garbage cans in the garage, now's the time to empty them.
- Open the garage door if it's not already open and grab your push broom to sweep. Begin by moving all that dirt and dust from the back of your garage toward the open door and outside where it belongs. You may want to wear a mask while you do this. Thanks to the width of a push broom, this job should go fairly quickly. (Of course, the ecofriendly approach and good-for-you-workout approach is pushing that broom, but perhaps your body isn't up to that chore today or you just don't have the time. In that case, you may want to use your tool system's battery-powered shop blower. In a perfect world, you always use the broom. But the world isn't perfect, so sometimes the blower wins.)
- Take a look around: Does the floor need more cleaning? Then use a hose, mop, or power washer to spray it down.

HL Tip: Here's an oldie-but-goodie storage idea: Put up pegboard—available today in wood, plastic, and metal, plus many colors. When installing, be sure to leave at least a half-inch gap between the pegboard and the wall; this space will accommodate the hooks from which you can hang all manner of tools. Plus, you can add baskets and shelves right onto the pegboard for more storage. Beware: Using pegboard can be addictive; soon you'll want an entire garage wall dedicated to it—and who could blame you?

- To remove any remaining oil spills or other stains, get scrubbing with a mild dish soap or citric acid and water plus a Tampico or coir brush.
- Done! Now kick back and relax. It's time to figure out how many friends you can host in your garage for that Halloween party.

The Ten-Minute Clean: Garage

It's the first beautiful spring weekend and you want to get those bikes out of the garage, pump up the tires, and ride. Do it! Then next weekend, when it's a bit rainy but you don't want to clean the whole house, invite the neighbors over for a potluck, a picnic, or a frozen pizza in the garage. Of course, you'll need to back out your vehicle(s). If you've got a boat in there, however, consider inviting the neighbors to climb on board for dinner. First, though, you'll need ten minutes to clean your garage.

- Grab that corn broom and knock down all those wintry cobwebs.
- Next, if you've got any trash cans in the garage, empty them to make way for items from your dinner. A friend keeps three labeled containers on hand in his garage: one for garbage, one for bottles and cans, and one for compost. He just pulls them out every time his family entertains outdoors.
- Now open that garage door if it's not already open and sweep the floor with your push broom or blow the dust out with your shop blower.
- Last, fill up that galvanized tub with ice and drinks. Ready!

My Ten-Minute Cleaning Playlist: Garage (Upbeat)
- "Go West" by the Pet Shop Boys (5:04)
- "Little Red Corvette" by Prince (5:03)

My Ten-Minute Cleaning Playlist: Garage (Mellow)
- "Like a Motorway" by Saint Etienne (5:42)
- "I Feel It Coming" by the Weeknd (4:29)

A TO Z: THINGS NOT TO STORE IN YOUR GARAGE

Apples: I know—Mom or Grandma used to wrap up each perfect apple, fresh from the orchard, in newspaper and then tuck them all into a box in the garage. But don't bother. If the too-warm or too-cool temperatures don't ruin them, the bugs or mice will find them and feast. Instead, store your apples in one of your refrigerator's crisper drawers—the perfect place for apples.

Art: Paintings belong on your walls or tucked away in a closet. You don't want all those Renoirs, Warhols, and finger-paint masterpieces cracking or flaking due to fluctuating temperatures.

Bedding: Like you, mice love curling up on bedding, sleeping bags, and stuffed animals. Unfortunately, they also like to eat the bedding and leave small signs of their visits.

Birth certificates, medical records, and passports: Store these important papers in a fireproof and waterproof document box in your home. These are too important to leave to the vagaries of vermin and insects.

Books: While mice don't read books (not even *Stuart Little*), they do love to shred them, making nests for their babies. Meanwhile, insects such as beetles, cockroaches, silverfish, and others like to eat the paper and the glue used in book bindings. Instead, keep books inside or, if you're done with them, add them to a Little Free Library or donate them.

Cardboard boxes: Cardboard is no match for the wildlife found in your garage. To fend off those critters, use plastic storage containers, galvanized buckets with lids, and glass jars for small items.

Carpet and rugs: Moisture and odors found in garages negatively affect these items, although rodents and pests don't seem to mind. For all three reasons, keep carpets and rugs indoors or donate any extras.

Clothing: See note after "Bedding." The same holds true for clothes.

Electronics: Fluctuating temperatures and electronics are never a good mix. Enough said.

Firewood: Lighting that fire in your fireplace won't seem nearly as romantic when beetles, centipedes, and millipedes scurry across the floor. Unfortunately, insects hitchhike on firewood brought into your garage and then into your home. Instead, keep firewood stacked, preferably a few inches off the ground, under an overhang, and set away from your house to provide airflow.

Food: Anything edible belongs in your kitchen or pantry—away from heat and humidity, and away from hungry unwanted visitors. (That includes humans. On a walk down their street, a friend's nephews, ages four and six, saw a freezer in a neighbor's garage and helped themselves to a couple of Popsicles. Too bad they returned home still licking the incriminating evidence!)

Fragile items: If it would be upsetting for Grandma and Grandpa's crystal glasses or Auntie Mae's Venetian glass paperweights to crack or even break, then they don't belong in a garage. Instead, put those items on display in your home or pack them away with paper shreds from your shredder or recycled packaging you've kept from purchases. Storing them in the garage, where accidents and frigid temperatures happen, is only asking for trouble.

Oily rags and other hazardous materials: Don't risk a fire. Instead, place the oily rag in an old can or a sealable bag, fill with water, and close. Then dispose of these containers and any other hazardous materials as is recommended by your county.

Paint: Store indoors, away from freezing and hot temperatures, and away from children. Paint can last up to a decade. But if you know that you'll never need a certain paint again, then recycle it (plenty of places are listed online); or donate it to a local theater, nonprofit, or community center. If it's latex paint, remove the lid and let the paint dry; then dispose of it in the trash. Or if it's oil paint, dispose of it, like any other hazardous material, as is recommended by your county.

Pet food: Unless it's in a metal container with a tight-fitting lid, keep Gus and Sadie's food indoors. You're not buying those bags of pet food for Mickey, Minnie, and Despereaux.

Photographs: Don't even think about storing these in the garage, where moisture and humidity can cause great harm. After all, that snapshot of you in eighth grade is priceless.

Propane tanks: While it's unlikely, propane tanks can and do explode. Instead, store them in a dry, well-ventilated outdoor space, away from your home.

Soap: What don't mice eat? This is yet another item they devour.

Wine: Place wine bottles on a rack indoors or (if you're fancy) in a wine refrigerator. Out in the garage, wine's chemistry can change with varying temperatures. And no one wants to drink to that!

CHAPTER 10

SUSTAINABILITY

LESS IS MORE

We can't expect the world to get better by itself. We have to create something we can leave the next generation.

—Gwen Ifill

Years ago, I was driving home from college when I turned a corner and, suddenly, stretched out before me was a breathtakingly beautiful expanse of Kentucky bluegrass. Unlike a mown lawn, this field had been allowed to grow upward of three feet tall, and there at the top of each blade was a cluster of the tiny blue flowers that give the plant its name. This vivid sky-blue meadow lay beneath an actual sky of blue and was wrapped up in a bow of Kentucky's ubiquitous white horse-farm fencing. I'll never forget it.

Whenever I revisit the epic poem "Kentucky Is My Land" by Jesse Stuart, that scene comes to mind. So too do oak trees, moss, and the woodsy view from my mom's deck. I was born and raised in Kentucky, and it was my home for well over twenty years.

For the past two decades, I've made my home much farther north—in Minnesota, another beautiful state. Here residents and visitors find more than ten thousand lakes, undulating farm fields, and, in its northeast, the Boundary Waters Canoe Area Wilderness (BWCAW), a million acres that include moose, black bears, wolves, otters, and, of course, hundreds of lakes.

The BWCAW can teach us a lot about sustainability—annual canoeists say no place on Earth feels more like home than this backcountry. They also know by heart its "leave no trace" principles, which help minimize their impact and keep the area "pristine and wild." And while I'm more camp than camper, I've always loved that phrase: It reminds me that I'm a citizen of the world, and I need to do my part.

Even my love of shopping, surprisingly, reinforced caring for the Earth from an early age. Not too far from my home was Stone & Thomas, a local department store that, in the 1980s, adopted a new logo of evergreen trees and the slogan: Saving the world is up to us all. They even began using recycled paper to create their bags and boxes. That too made an impact on me, especially as I grew up in a place of incredible natural beauty.

The world is our home. Caring for it is up to us. And that means our individual homes too, including our consumption of goods and our cleaning methods.

Doing More with Less

Too often we use myriad chemical products when one or two simple, natural options deliver a better result. Have you ever used a chemical bathroom cleaner only to watch a big drip land on a rug or, worse, a favorite garment? Then you use another cleaner or maybe two to remove that first product? Or perhaps you don't like the smell of a certain cleaner, so then you spray a room freshener to cover up that scent?

Most of us have dozens of cleaning products tucked under our sinks. Some we use regularly, some accumulate dust, and some are eventually chucked into the garbage because they didn't live up to their marketing hype. Did you know that experts actually recommend not storing chemical cleaners under the sink? They're dangerous to kids and pets, their fumes can build up, and, if spilled, they can create a dangerous chemical reaction. I say, don't buy most of them in the first place.

When we choose to rely on simple, natural cleaners like our 50/50 vinegar-water solution, we're being sustainable. We're buying fewer products. We're reusing containers, refilling our spray bottles from giant jugs. And we're using simple ingredients, so when a few drops of vinegar fall, there's no harm, no foul, and no mystery chemicals that can hurt you, your loved ones, your home, or your environment. Our home should be our sanctuary, where it's clean—and safe.

Doing Due Diligence

That said, just because a cleaner is labeled ecofriendly or green doesn't mean that's actually true. Companies that make such claims rarely suffer consequences when those promises are misleading or downright false. That's called greenwashing and it's common. You'd be surprised at how many major brands (yes, likely the ones popping into your head right now) market products as natural and nontoxic when their ingredients are anything but.

And it's not just misleading information about cleaners—false claims have been made by a multitude of companies. Here are some examples:

- A business can misrepresent its carbon footprint by not accurately revealing the amount of greenhouse gases their company generates.
- A car company can use emissions-cheating software to say its vehicles operate cleanly.
- A manufacturer could say its products are purely plant based when in fact they're not.
- A skin-care brand could promise its sunscreen is kind to reefs, but it turns out that colorful coral is still under attack.
- A company could give its new line of products an ecofriendly name, like TreeGarden Greenly Green Toothpaste (now in Pumpkin Spice!), so its target audience assumes it's environmentally sound even though it's not even close. (Remember that 1970s ecological horror movie, *Soylent Green*? Even its cannibalistic product had *green* in the name.)
- A company with an environmentally friendly reputation is purchased, but the new owner could reformulate its products, making them not even close to green.

- Even some pet-product companies can't be trusted—one claimed its waste bags for pet poo were recyclable. The hitch? You'd have to pack up all those small green bags (with their precious cargo) in your suitcase on your next vacation to a country where processors actually can recycle them. I guess we all need to read the fine print.

What products do we use regularly that we haven't given a second thought to until now? Consider those dense white sponges used for cleaning. Made of a compound called formaldehyde-melamine-sodium bisulfite copolymer, they're linked in some studies to microplastics in our waterways. And purchasers are warned to wear gloves whenever using them to ward off skin burns and rashes. Rather than take the risk, how about we skip using those—just in case?

And what about paper towels? Think about this: When you're cleaning with paper towels, you're actually creating more waste. Instead, rely on rags made of old clothes, old towels, or old sheets, which are more effective anyway. I also use bar towels—I'm obsessed with them, in fact. Designed to clean up spills at a bar, they're super durable and likely ten times more absorbent than paper towels. Simply wash and dry any of these items and they can be kept in circulation for months or even years.

As consumers, we must be wary. Businesses know we care about the environment or they wouldn't make these claims in the first place. But companies that lie about being Earth-friendly are counting on consumers' lives being too busy for them to pay attention. They don't want us to check out their green credentials online or to turn those products around and read their ingredients lists. Or they hope we're fooled when we see the words *perfume* or *fragrance*—not realizing that a cauldron of chemicals can be hidden under such a generic term.

The next time you're at the store and you're tempted to buy a green-labeled product, take a gander at that ingredients list and check out the claims online. Then determine for yourself whether it's a product that you want in your house. And if it's not truly ecofriendly, don't be afraid to stand up to that company and be counted among other green consumers. If we demand more Earth-friendly products, maybe companies will provide them.

Be aware: There are general environmental warnings against using products, cleaning and otherwise, with carbon, nitrogen, phosphorus, and sulfur outside of your home. Once again, remember to read those labels.

And if you'd like to do your part, make a commitment to using natural cleaners like vinegar and water as often as possible. They're not only safe and easy, both for our houses and our planet, but they're also wildly effective. And bonus—vinegar is cheap. What's not to love?

Making Things Last

Something that gets me madder than a wet hen (as we say in the South) is when people buy things they don't really love and then replace them a year or two later. Call me a thoughtful consumer, but I like to dwell on significant purchases for a good long while before I buy. And then I take good care of them, ensuring they last as long as possible.

When we moved into our house, for example, I knew exactly which chairs I wanted to add to our den, but I couldn't find them right away. Eventually, I spotted them online and made the purchase. Fourteen years later I still love them.

The same holds true for our sofas; I'll never get rid of them—I'll only reupholster. And it took me eight months until I found the right carpet for our staircase, but the additional cost of a pricier floor covering is a bargain compared to replacing cheaper carpeting every few years. After all, the real cost is often labor, especially on those staircases.

Thinking back to furniture, I'm often thankful for my friend Louise's great aunt Alma, or Al as everyone called her. She purchased a tall and graceful writing desk, or secretary, and it's been passed down to loved ones throughout the generations. Eventually my mom will give it to me. Passing along beloved objects is sustainability too.

Or consider clothes. Rather than regularly buying fast fashion, what makes more sense from your wallet's standpoint is investing in high-quality essentials for year-round use and buying a few popular items each season. If you really love your garments, both classic and trendy, you'll be more motivated to take care of them and make them last. In sum, you'll be buying both more thoughtfully and less.

The thrifting trend elates me—and not just because I sell vintage clothing at Mona Williams. Thrifters keep great clothes and great household items out of landfills and enjoy them anew. For my part, I've been collecting dishes in the Pfaltzgraff Farmers Market pattern for thirty years—from garage sales, yard sales, and online. They're not expensive pieces, but it's a thrill every time I add one to my collection and then share it during a party or get-together.

An unlikely advocate for thrifting, Elizabeth Taylor once said, "It's not the having, it's the getting." And that's so true. The anticipation of searching for and then finding that special item is way more fun than immediate gratification, according to behavioral psychologists. I recently added a sparkly 1970s Christmas tree topper to my collection—I'd been looking for one for at least fifteen years. (Ruby had one when I was growing up and I'd always wanted one.) With thrifting, you're both finding something you absolutely love—and you're saving something. Thrifting is also sustainability.

Thoughtful purchasing goes even deeper: If you accumulate the things you really love, rather than the things you just kind of like, I believe you'll live a better life. And I mean that to be the case no matter the price. There are plenty of times where you might love the garage sale vase better than the new one at the discount store or the museum shop. Buy the one you really love or you're likely to stay on the lookout for yet another one. Or perhaps you have to save up for that leather jacket you've fallen for, but keep in mind that you'll wear it for decades. Perhaps you'll even gift it to a child or grandchild. (If it's a bit pricey, feel free to shred that receipt—like I do—so you don't have to think about it again.)

House Love is certainly not a prepper guide, and I don't advocate living off the grid, growing all your own food, and weaving your own clothes. That's not realistic for most of us. Instead, this book counsels choosing and using safe products as often as you can, being thoughtful as you make decisions about your house and its contents, and caring for the planet however and wherever you can. If all of us adopt small changes, they'll add up. In the meantime, you'll feel better, you'll live better, and you might even be happier. I firmly believe that living a greener life is living a better life.

Caring for Our Homes

Minnesota is my home. Kentucky is my home. (In fact, I often tell people that I'm a little Yankee and a little y'all.) My house is also my home. Home is the box you live in, and it's everything around that box you live in. It's our whole world, our entire planet. The point of sustainability is you're taking care of home.

Not long ago, I went back home (there's that word again) to Kentucky to visit family. I was sitting on that deck of my mom and step-dad's house. They actually live in the home my mom grew up in—talk about sustainability—and it was a beautiful day. The hills were all around, the grass and trees were swaying, and everywhere I looked was green and lush. It reminded me of playing in nature as a kid. I loved running pell-mell into the woods and exploring with my cousin Loretta. We'd hike, pick berries and wildflowers, and climb trees. But my favorite thing to do was play in the creek at Granny Martha's house. On hot summer days, we'd wade, skip rocks, splash, and even lie down in the spring-fed shallow creek.

I was dwelling on those memories when it suddenly struck me—these experiences are exactly what we're trying to save when we talk about sustainability. It's why we take care of the planet. It's why we value the natural world and want it to last. It's why we wade, hike, canoe, forage, bike, ski, and roll down hills. We want to enjoy it today and preserve it for the generations who come after.

And if Kentucky's landscape doesn't inspire you, maybe Minnesota's Boundary Waters do, or South Dakota's Badlands, Utah's Arches National Park, the Appalachians out east, the Rockies out west, or picturesque harbors wherever you find them. Or maybe your scenes are more far-flung—Norway's fjords, Peru's Sacred Valley, or Vietnam's Ban Gioc Falls.

No matter where nature makes your heart sing, isn't that worth cleaning with natural products, using sustainable scrub brushes, pulling down your shades to cut the electricity you use in the summer, buying and caring for only those items you truly love, and a hundred other small but significant practices?

Yes, I think so too.

CHAPTER 11

REMEMBER

MAKE YOURSELF AT HOME

To us, our house was not unsentient matter—it had a heart,
and a soul, and eyes to see us with; and approvals, and
solicitudes, and deep sympathies; it was of us, and we were
in its confidence, and lived in its grace and in the peace of its
benediction. We never came home from an absence that its
face did not light up and speak out its eloquent welcome—and
we could not enter it unmoved.

—Mark Twain

As kids, lots of us draw a house as a square with a triangle roof, a rectangular door, and square windows (plus maybe a circle sun and some green grass lines scattered about). But few homes actually look like that. People live in all kinds of places: apartments, condos, townhomes, tiny houses, big houses, mansions, tents, RVs, houseboats, sailboats, and many more types of dwellings all over the world. You can lay your head pretty much anywhere. (As a kid, I was certain a pillow fort was all I needed.)

This book's title, *House Love: A Joyful Guide to Cleaning, Organizing, and Loving the Home You're In*, was chosen deliberately. A house, in whatever form it takes, is what you live in. But add love and you've suddenly got a home.

Imagine it's moving day and you haul your things, your boxes, and your bags into those empty spaces, all new to you. By introducing items that reflect your interests, hobbies, and passions, you transform those empty spaces, over time, into your house. Then add care for those things you love, those spaces you live in, and, most especially, those people (and pets) there (whether they live with you day in and day out or just visit)—and one day, it's not just your house but your home.

I hope by now, as we wrap things up, you've found a handful (or maybe even dozens) of ways to show love to your spaces. Like I said, anyplace can be home. The important thing—even if you aspire to a bigger, better, or different home someday—is to love the one you're presently in, just like the book's subtitle says.

Ross and I had been living in our current house for over a year when we decided to throw a New Year's Day party. By then, we'd painted our vestibule a vivid orange, carpeted our stairs, selected furniture that—by design—could transform our entryway into a dining room whenever needed, and given our living room and den a sparkly nighttime vibe. We'd hung our favorite art, outfitted our bedrooms, and remodeled our bathroom. The construction dust was long gone and the moving boxes had been nicely recycled or shared with friends who were also moving. We were ready for a party.

I'd just spent the holidays with my family in Kentucky, and I returned eager to share foods and recipes from home with friends and family. That's where we found our theme: Our entire shindig's spread was Southern, including appetizers like Tennessee Sin (a cheesy dip whose name is on point—see page 205 for the recipe), butternut squash dip, pimento cheese, and plenty of breads and crackers, plus festive libations.

As our house filled up with people from all areas of our lives, I realized that our house worked: Our elegant kitchen was the perfect place to serve guests as we pulled hot pans of country ham and sausage balls out of the oven and placed them on the countertops. Our friends and family were able to move effortlessly from kitchen to living room to den, plus upstairs and downstairs, delightedly touring our new house and enjoying all the things we'd filled it with, including holiday decorations virtually everywhere they looked.

Everyone seemed happy and at ease, hanging out on the landing, chatting with friends in the living room and den, or taking seats in our dining room/entryway to enjoy slices of red velvet cake.

As the open house wound down well into the evening, I walked each guest to the front door, sharing a last laugh or a quick hug. And when I closed the door for the final time that night, I knew: I was home.

CALENDAR OF CLEAN

Lots of publications offer rundowns of cleaning projects to do each month, such as cleaning out the junk drawer in January, organizing your file cabinet in April (I guess because of taxes), and cleaning your basement's copper pipes in September. (Really, that's not a thing, although a friend's brother likes to do that.)

My list is a lot more commonsensical and a little more fun. Plus, I throw in some shopping tips along the way—I have worked in retail for eons, after all. No doubt I'll be updating this list in the years to come and will share online as it makes sense to do so.

Feel free to write your own tasks in the margins. It's your book after all! You might have other favorite things you like to do at various times of the year—say, dig out and clean the crank ice cream maker in May so it's ready for June, or start cleaning out your garage in June for your annual sale in July. (If that last idea pertains to you, do send me a note on the date, especially if you live in Minnesota. I love garage sales.)

January

Baby, it's cold outside. (Or pretend it is.) Soup is simmering in the slow cooker. And you've got enough willpower to resist that novel someone gifted you or that new binge-worthy TV show until later tonight.

Now's the perfect time to deep-clean any neglected spaces:

- It's the darkest month of the year—that suggests dusting all your light fixtures and swapping out any bulbs that are kaput. After turning off all the lights, grab that duster, a few new bulbs, and a stepladder you can easily move from room to room, and you'll be done in no time.
- If you've got seasonal décor to store away until next year, you might want to clean out and/or reorganize your attic or storage space.
- By January, it's likely that you've figured out which winter clothes you no longer need. Why not simplify your mornings by keeping on hand only the items you really love? Donate the clothes you don't want to a thrift store or sell them online.
- Clean those out-of-sight, out-of-mind spaces: the medicine cabinet, yes, that junk drawer, behind and under the refrigerator (throwing out those dusty pretzels will help prevent mice from taking up residence), under the sink, under the bed(s), and all those closets: hallway, bathroom, mudroom, etc.
- A new year often brings a new reason to simplify: What other items do you need or not need in your life? Pick up the former at after-holiday sales, and donate or throw away the latter. Ah, it feels so good to start the year organized!
- Shopping: Need to refresh your bedding? January tends to offer the best deals.

February

If there were a Super Bowl of cleaning, it would be a punch bowl filled with vinegar and rags. Now's the month to show your home some love—it is the month of valentines, after all—by moving up on the to-do list those things that are a tad tedious.

- Start with what's underfoot: Steam your floors, clean the grout, wax any hardwood floors, and touch up any floor scratches.
- After your valentine cookies are done baking, it's probably time to clean the oven with water, vinegar, and baking soda. (For the deets, see page 87.)
- On a day that feels like spring, open up a few windows for fifteen minutes to freshen up your house and get rid of stale air. (Perhaps you do this on an evening when your husband is out at a concert to ensure you won't hear these words being yelled from another room: "Are we paying to heat the outdoors?!" This example may or may not be taken from my own life.)
- Once again, consider grabbing that duster and a stepladder, and then moving from room to room, dusting the tops of kitchen cabinets, tall pieces of furniture, and more.
- Speaking of large furniture, enlist a friend or partner to help you move them. Then sweep or vacuum under them—plus retrieve those missing Legos, random change, and maybe even that dog toy that's been lost forever.
- If you take this opportunity to move your furniture around, you may need to get rid of those impressions on your carpet. Just place ice cubes on the impressions, let them melt over a couple of hours, blot the dampened impressions with a clean rag and then use your fingers to fluff the carpet back up. By the time the carpet dries, the impressions will be gone.
- In honor of Valentine's Day, consider doing the chore that your partner or roommate or child likes least. (If you're lucky, maybe they'll do yours too.)
- Shopping: Need new flowerpots? Buy them now while the selection is best.

March

Spring is coming, and that means your entryway is going to get "mud-luscious" and "puddle wonderful," à la E. E. Cummings. This room needs lots of extra attention.

- **Your front door:** Clean it from top to bottom, and both sides. If there's a window in your front door, eliminate any fingerprints with a squirt of your vinegar-water solution and a swipe. Perhaps it's even time to repaint—the same color or maybe orange like mine.
- **Your entryway closet:** After a long winter, depending on where you live, those heavy coats need laundering and putting away until next year. (If you live in the frigid north like me, this task should happen in May. Not kidding.)
- **Your shoe tray:** Time to swap the snow boots for the rain boots (again, this is delayed until April or May in the north) and add a towel or two for wiping Bo's paws.
- **Your entryway floor:** Scrub the grout, steam the tile, and refresh that rug, whether by washing or replacing.

April

Finally—it's time for spring cleaning—before the weather is so nice that you're practically living outside. I'd recommend flipping back through each chapter and cleaning one or two rooms per weekend. By the end of the month, your house will gleam. Here are some extra tips:

- When it's warm enough to open the windows, dust everything, including your window treatments, windowsills, and books.

- Then vacuum every room to suck up all that dust.
- If you can, carry your area rugs outside and shake or beat them. If not, flip them over inside and vacuum their backsides.
- If you've got any firewood left, make another winter fire or two, light your candles, and enjoy a few last chilly nights full of hygge.
- Take stock of any lingering winter foods in your pantry or cupboards. Got half a dozen cans of tomatoes, wild rice, or creamed corn? It's obviously time to make more soup or a few cozy casseroles. As soon as it's summer, you'll want to be outside grilling.
- Shopping: Need any grill utensils? Ensure you have what you need now so you're ready on that first day you've got a hankering for kebobs or burgers.

May

If you have kids, May is arguably the busiest month of the year, with recitals, performances, sporting competitions, picnics, graduations, and more. Maybe cut yourself some slack inside and pay a bit more attention to your outdoor living spaces. After all, it's likely that in many places mosquitoes haven't yet arrived in full force, the temperature is near perfect, and the spring flowers are blooming.

- Depending on where you live, it's likely time (if you haven't already) to bring your houseplants outside. That's when I move my lime tree, Brian Jones, from the bathroom to the deck. Be sure too to clean any spaces indoors where those plants sat.
- Now take your cleaning outside. Scrub your grill so it's ready. Get out the hose and spray down the garage, the deck, and/or the patio.
- Update what's in your car—swap out that shovel and ice scraper for a picnic basket and portable chairs for baseball games or camping.
- Scrub the stains off any patio furniture.

- Call the chimney service and get your home on the summer schedule, so you're ready for the fall.

June

Maybe this is the summer that you plan to replace a few windows, add more landscaping, expand your garden, or stain your deck—again. Whatever's planned, you likely don't want to while away your hours inside. But if there's a rainy day or two, consider these ideas:

- If you've got kids, now that school's out, give them a day or two to clean their bedrooms, chuck those old papers and notebooks, and start fresh. And as long as they're dusting, maybe dust off that library card and head to the local library for a stack of summery books.
- Give some love to the kitchen, clearing space for favorite items from the farmer's market and for summery snacks and lunches.
- Move your summer clothes into your closet and pack away your freshly laundered winter clothes.
- Pull out all the fans and wipe them down with your vinegar-water solution. If you're unable to wipe down the blades of a boxed fan, use canned air to remove the dust. For ceiling fans, gently wrap an old towel around a blade and pull away to remove the mother lode of dust; repeat with each of the blades. Then when most of the dust is gone, use the vinegar-water solution to wipe down the blades again.

July

It's va-cay time! If you're out of town, you can't very well clean your home. And if you're doing a stay-cation (my frequent preference), you shouldn't be cleaning either, especially if the weather happens to be beautiful. That said, you could put a few things on your to-do list:

- If you're grabbing your suitcases this month, perhaps it's time to clean out the closet where they're stored.
- If you have air-conditioning, be sure to change out the filters again. (No doubt they've gotten lots of use so far this season.)
- Carpets need some care? Now's a good time to shampoo them—after all, they'll dry so much faster with the windows open or the air-conditioning running.
- Shopping: This is the perfect month to start thinking about fall—yep, school clothes are back in stores.

August

It's summer's last hurrah. Keep your home tidy, but cut yourself some slack. There are still pools to swim in, bike rides and hikes to take, marshmallows to roast. Everything else can wait.

That said, if redoing a kid's room has been on your to-do list, now's a great time, right before school starts. Doing so also doesn't have to be hard: Repaint, refresh the bedding (and maybe the mattress), change up the posters, and get a new area rug. Check, check, check, and check!

September

If you've got young kids, life gets super busy in September. And even without kids, schedules change, projects pile up, the social calendar fills. You'll want to crank up the cozy with any downtime you can grab. And with temps dropping, now's just the time:

- Clean your light fixtures—it's likely they're super dusty from having your windows open all summer long. Double-check that all your bulbs are working.
- Turn your attention to your entryway(s) again. Ensure you've got hooks and/or hangers for coats, a basket for hats and mittens, and a tray for boots.
- Deep-clean your den and living room, including vacuuming the sofa(s). No doubt you'll be spending a lot of time there.
- Vacuum your mattress(es). Wash all the blankets before adding them to your bed(s). And swap out those crisp summer sheets for flannel.
- If you took up your rugs for the summer, return them to your floors. They'll feel good during chillier winter days.
- Shopping: Stock up on candles. Maybe you need some spicy fall ones now and a Fraser fir one for December? A lovely flicker and a beautiful scent can help create a bit of serenity whenever it's needed.

October

Fall is getting in full swing. Now's the perfect time to focus on two disparate spaces—your kitchen and your garage.

- Clean your kitchen, but stretch out the process over a week if need be, cleaning every pot and pan, every cupboard, every surface—plus the stove and the refrigerator. Pull out that slow cooker, those new cooking gadgets you bought on vacation, and your favorite fall recipes. It's time to start cooking in earnest again.

- Take stock of your spices and herbs. Perhaps a few are a bit old and need replacing. You might also buy a couple of potted herbs (or pot up an herb or two from your garden), so you can keep using fresh herbs all winter long.

- Do an inventory of your cooking tools. Do you have your pumpkin-carving tools ready? Do you have a candy thermometer on hand for that divinity recipe you want to try? Thanksgiving is right around the corner—do you have a turkey baster and a meat thermometer?

- Get your garage ready for colder weather: Put away the bikes and the toys, pull out the snow shovels, and rearrange your storage so you can actually park again in your garage (and the kids can ride around on their trikes in the garage during midwinter). Stock up on sand (preferably) or road salt to help with traction on ice. And while you're at it, deep-clean your car, washing and vacuuming it—or take it to a full-service car wash.

November

- It's nearly go time! Early in the month, especially if you're hosting guests or entertaining, check these to-do items off your list to make your weeks go smoothly: Deep-clean any entertaining spaces: entryway, living room, and dining room. If you currently use any of these spaces as a home office, figure out a conversion plan now so you don't have to do so in a hurry when the time comes.

- Clean the guest bedroom if need be, including dusting, vacuuming, and laundering all the bedding.

- Polish the silverware, including any serving pieces and candlesticks if you plan to use them.
- Wash all your serving pieces. If they've been on display in your china cabinet and you previously washed them with ammonia (to make them gleam), wash them again, this time without the ammonia.
- Freshly wash and starch all your table linens, including any table-cloths, table runners, and cloth napkins, to prepare for holiday hosting events.
- Consider wiping down the walls and shampooing the carpets as well.
- And if you feel particularly inspired, touch up those spots on the wall with paint.
- Shopping: While Black Friday and Cyber Monday used to be single-day events, now great deals are available all month long. Also, early November days bring great deals on children's costumes they can use all year.

December

This isn't the month for deep cleaning. Rely on the ten-minute cleans and just aim to keep your home tidy. A little dust isn't fatal. (Plus, is it dust or is it soot from Santa—or that magic dust that makes the reindeer fly?) You're plenty busy already—entertaining, shopping, cooking, doing dishes, and washing table and bed linens. Be kind to yourself during the holidays. Cut yourself some slack. It's the memories with loved ones that count, not how perfect your house looks.

HOUSE LOVE'S RECIPES (WORTH EVERY STAIN)

n *Laundry Love*, I included lots of delicious, stain-inducing recipes. They were a big hit. So here are more favorites, this time inspired by various spaces in my home. Enjoy!

Entryway

When I was growing up, my mom always made guests feel welcome the moment they arrived. Today, I follow her lead, often taking a guest's jacket and offering a beverage so they can settle in. I've provided two options—one for cooler weather and one for hot summer days.

CRANBERRY TEA

Serves 14

4 cups fresh cranberries

3½ quarts water

12 whole cloves

4 cinnamon sticks,
  approximately 3 inches long

Juice from 2 lemons

Juice from 2 oranges

2 cups sugar

Place the cranberries, water, cloves, and cinnamon sticks in a saucepan, and simmer on medium heat for 12 minutes. Add the lemon and orange juices plus the sugar. Increase the heat to medium-high and stir continuously until the mixture is just boiling. Let cool off a bit but serve hot.

LEMONADE BOURBON SLUSH

Serves a summery crowd of roughly 18

1 (12-ounce) can frozen
  lemonade, thawed

1 (12-ounce) can frozen orange
  juice, thawed

½ cup sugar

6 cups water

3 cups bourbon

7UP or other lemon-lime soda

In a large bowl, mix together the lemonade, orange juice, sugar, water, and bourbon and then freeze until slushy. To serve, add 3 tablespoons of the mixture to each glass of roughly 8 ounces. Then fill each glass with 7UP.

WILMA'S BLACKBERRY CAKE

When you're a guest, you might bring a bottle of wine or a bouquet of flowers to your host. My mom brings this decadent, old-fashioned cake, one she's locally famous for. Honestly, people in the know are waiting on the other side of the door just hoping she's brought along her signature cake. She'd even make it for fundraisers—one fan purchased it repeatedly for grand sums. My mom uses pecans, but you might consider adding black walnuts as that's a more Appalachian choice for this Southern dessert.

Serves 12 to 15

CAKE

1 cup (2 sticks) unsalted butter, at room temperature, plus more for greasing the pan

2 cups sugar

4 large eggs

1 teaspoon ground cinnamon

1 teaspoon ground allspice

1 teaspoon ground nutmeg

½ teaspoon ground cloves

Dash of kosher salt

1 teaspoon baking soda

1 cup buttermilk

2 cups all-purpose flour

2 cups fresh or frozen blackberries, undrained if frozen

½ cup pecans or black walnuts, coarsely chopped

FROSTING

3 cups packed light brown sugar

2 tablespoons light corn syrup

3 tablespoons unsalted butter

Dash of kosher salt

¾ cup heavy cream

1 teaspoon vanilla extract

Preheat the oven to 350°F. Grease a 9 × 13-inch baking pan with butter.

Make the cake: In a large bowl with an electric mixer or using a stand mixer, cream together the butter and sugar until light and fluffy. Then add the eggs, cinnamon, allspice, nutmeg, cloves, and salt and mix thoroughly.

In a separate bowl, whisk together the baking soda and buttermilk. Alternate adding the buttermilk mixture and the flour into the butter-sugar-spice mixture, beating well after each addition. Add the blackberries and pecans and mix until just combined.

Pour the mixture into the prepared pan. Bake for 25 to 30 minutes, until a toothpick inserted into the center comes out clean.

Make the frosting: In a saucepan, place all the ingredients and stir to blend. Bring to a boil over medium heat, stirring occasionally, and cover for 3 minutes while it continues to boil. Uncover and continue to cook until a soft ball forms (238°F on a candy thermometer). Remove the pan from the heat and allow it to cool for 3 minutes. Beat the mixture with an electric mixer or by hand until it becomes thick but spreadable (it will lose its gloss).

Spread the frosting over the cooled cake with a butter knife or offset spatula. If the frosting is too thick, add a tablespoon of hot water to loosen it. Dipping the knife in hot water will also help make spreading the frosting easier.

Living Room

TENNESSEE SIN

First of all, you have to love the name. Baked inside of a loaf of bread, this cheesy, gooey appetizer is aptly titled for its decadent deliciousness. I got this oh-so-1970s recipe from my mom when I first started hosting parties. It's now so popular that some friends' RSVPs depend on knowing if I'm making this. (I don't blame them.) It's a great appetizer if you're throwing a fete, but it's simple enough to make at the last minute for a few friends. In fact, it turns every gathering into something special. And again, that name—so perfect.

Serves 12

2 (16-ounce) loaves of French bread

8 ounces cream cheese, at room temperature

8 ounces sour cream

16 ounces cheddar cheese, shredded

½ cup chopped cooked ham

⅓ cup chopped green onions

¼ teaspoon Worcestershire sauce

Dash of ground paprika

(recipe continues)

Preheat the oven to 350°F.

Slice off the top fourth of one bread loaf and set it aside. Hollow out the bottom of the loaf, leaving a 1-inch shell. Cut the reserved bread top, the insides of the loaf you've removed, and the entire remaining loaf into 1-inch cubes. Bake the hollow bread and the cubes on a sheet pan until lightly browned, approximately 5 minutes.

In a large bowl with an electric mixer or using a stand mixer, beat the cream cheese at medium speed until smooth, then add the sour cream, cheese, ham, green onions, and Worcestershire sauce until combined. Spoon the mixture into the bread shell, wrap the loaf in heavy-duty aluminum foil, and bake for 30 minutes.

Carefully remove the foil, sprinkle the top with paprika, and serve hot with the toasted bread cubes alongside.

THE ICONIC SAUSAGE BALLS

My mom never throws a party without serving this iconic party food. In fact, I'd guess they're in the repertoire of most Southern cooks. Fortunately, they're as easy to make as they are delectable, and you can bake them ahead, freeze them, and then throw them in the air fryer or oven for reheating. But why wait for a party? I often pack a few for my lunch.

Makes 30 balls

Butter, for greasing the baking sheets

1 pound ground spicy sausage, at room temperature

3 cups Bisquick (see Note) pancake and baking mix

8 ounces sharp cheddar cheese, shredded

3 tablespoons water

Preheat the oven to 400°F and grease two baking sheets with butter.

In a large bowl, mix together all the ingredients thoroughly. Using your hands, roll the mixture into 1½-inch balls and place them on the prepared baking sheets. Bake for 15 to 20 minutes, until no longer pink inside and browned on the outside.

Note: Did you know Bisquick, an indispensable product in Kentucky, is made by General Mills, which started in Minnesota? That's yet another connection between my childhood home and my current home state.

Dining Room

When I was growing up, Mom served all of these cookies in the dining room at Christmastime. This is, to my mind, how to celebrate the holiday—offering a cookie smorgasbord, plates and napkins stacked at the ready. Make one or make them all. Then dig in.

MOLLY'S SANTA'S WHISKERS

A little hint of cherry is a nice counterpoint to the crunch of this cookie. If you, like my mom, hate coconut, you can leave that out and they're still delicious. (Thanks, Suzanne, for letting me share this favorite! Mom and I have been baking and eating your mom's cookies since 1976—without the coconut.)

Makes 60 cookies

1 cup margarine, at room temperature
1 cup sugar
2 tablespoons whole milk
1 teaspoon vanilla extract

2½ cups all-purpose flour
¾ cup candied cherries, chopped (see Note)
½ cup pecans, chopped
¾ cup flaked coconut

Preheat the oven to 375°F. Line two baking sheets with parchment paper.

In a large bowl with an electric mixer or using a stand mixer, cream together the margarine and sugar until light and fluffy. Add

(recipe continues)

the milk and vanilla, followed by the flour, cherries, and nuts. Form the dough into two logs, each approximately 2 inches in diameter and 8 inches long. Roll the logs in the coconut, wrap each log in wax paper, and place them in the refrigerator to chill for at least 1 hour.

Remove the logs and cut them into ¼-inch slices. Place the slices on the prepared baking sheets about 1 inch apart. Bake for 12 minutes, until slightly brown. Allow the cookies to cool on the baking sheets for 2 minutes, then move them to a rack to cool completely.

Note: If you can't find candied cherries, drain some maraschino cherries and set them on a paper towel overnight. They must be completely dry before using.

GOLDEN SUGAR COOKIES

These drop sugar cookies are my absolute favorite. No contest.

Makes 36 cookies

2½ cups all-purpose flour
1 teaspoon baking soda
1 teaspoon cream of tartar
¼ teaspoon kosher salt

1 cup (2 sticks) unsalted butter, at room temperature
2½ teaspoons vanilla
2 cups sugar
3 large egg yolks

Preheat the oven to 350°F.

In a large bowl, sift together the flour, baking soda, cream of tartar, and salt; set aside.

In a separate large bowl with an electric mixer or using a stand mixer, cream together the butter and vanilla until light and fluffy. Now gradually add the sugar, creaming after each addition. Add 1 egg yolk at a time, beating after each addition. Gradually add the dry ingredients, beating after each addition until combined.

Form the dough into 1-inch balls. Place on two ungreased baking sheets 3 inches apart. Bake for 12 minutes, until slightly brown around the edges. Allow the cookies to cool on the baking sheets for 5 minutes, then move them to a rack to cool completely.

SPANISH LACE COOKIES

Fragile and special, lacy cookies stand out at any cookie swap.

Makes 48 cookies

2 cups (4 sticks) unsalted butter, at room temperature, plus more for greasing the baking sheets

1 cup granulated sugar

1 cup brown sugar

2 large eggs, separated

2½ cups old-fashioned oats

1 teaspoon baking powder

1 cup chopped walnuts

1 teaspoon vanilla extract

Preheat the oven to 350°F. Grease two baking sheets with butter.

In a large bowl with an electric mixer or using a stand mixer, cream together the butter and both sugars until light and fluffy. Whisk in the egg yolks until just combined.

In a separate medium bowl, stir together the oats and baking powder. Add the mixture to the wet ingredients and whisk to combine. Fold in the nuts and vanilla, and set the bowl aside.

In another medium bowl with an electric mixer or using a stand mixer, beat the egg whites until they reach the stiff peak stage, then gently fold them into the batter.

Drop teaspoonfuls of the dough about 3 inches apart on the prepared baking sheets. Bake for 7 to 8 minutes, until slightly brown. Allow the cookies to cool on the baking sheets for 2 minutes; then remove them carefully to a rack to cool completely.

Kitchen (Comfort Food That You Eat in the Kitchen)

CORNBREAD CASSEROLE

Whoever dreamed up this cornbread casserole is a genius. Packed with chicken, cheese, and jalapeños, this recipe is in my regular rotation. Pair it with a salad and you've got a great last-minute dinner for guests. Plus, while it's baking, you can do a couple ten-minute cleans. Talk about easy entertaining!

Serves 8

½ cup corn oil, plus more for the baking dish

1¼ cups yellow cornmeal, plus 3 tablespoons for the baking dish

1½ cups whole milk

1 (14.75-ounce) can cream-style corn

3 large eggs

2 teaspoons kosher salt

¾ teaspoon baking soda

4 cups shredded Mexican cheese blend

3 large boneless, skinless chicken breasts, cooked and shredded

½ cup pickled jalapeños (from a jar not a can), drained and sliced

½ cup fresh cilantro, chopped (optional)

2 tablespoons unsalted butter

Salsa, for serving

Sour cream, for serving

Preheat the oven to 350°F. Grease a 3-quart or 9 × 13-inch baking dish with oil. Sprinkle 3 tablespoons of the cornmeal on the bottom and sides of the pan. Bake the pan for 3 to 4 minutes and set aside to cool, keeping the oven on.

In a large bowl, whisk together the oil, milk, corn, eggs, salt, and baking soda. Add the remaining 1¼ cups cornmeal and stir until mixed. Pour half of the batter into the prepared baking dish.

Sprinkle the top with the cheese, chicken, jalapeños, and cilantro (if using). Pour in the rest of the batter.

Bake for roughly 1 hour, until a fork inserted into the center of the casserole comes out clean. Add butter to the top of the casserole and allow it to cool for 15 minutes. Serve with salsa and sour cream on the side.

PATRIC'S GRILLED CHEESE

I'd never heard of restaurant-quality grilled-cheese sandwiches until I started going to Ed and Fred's Desert Moon, a longtime Kentucky restaurant. Those visits inspired me to create my own grilled cheese—stuffing everything I love into it. My friend always requests this sandwich for his birthday, and let me just say, it's better than birthday cake (and probably has more calories). It's the stuff of legend. You'll wow your loved ones with this ultimate comfort food.

Makes 1 sandwich

3 bacon strips
½ apple, sliced
¼ white onion, sliced
3 tablespoons butter

2 slices rustic bread (I prefer onion rosemary)
1 slice cheddar cheese
1 slice Swiss cheese

In a large skillet, preferably cast iron, fry the bacon over medium heat until crisp. Set aside to drain on a plate lined with a paper towel.

Using the same pan with the drippings, cook the apple and onion slices until softened, about 5 minutes.

Use 1½ tablespoons of the butter to butter both sides of the bread slices and lay one slice in the same pan. Add the bacon to that slice, followed by the cheddar and Swiss cheese, apples, and onions. Then add the second slice of bread. Add the remaining 1½ tablespoons butter to the pan (unless you still have enough bacon drippings!). Now toast the sandwich in the skillet, flipping once, until each side is golden brown. Slice in half and serve.

Laundry Room

CLOTHESPIN COOKIES

I'd never even heard of these cookies until one of my customers told me about them. What a surprise and delight to discover! They're like little delicious cream horns but better. You'll need a pastry bag and a dozen wooden clothespins (the round ones, not the clips) to whip up a batch, and then, when you throw in your next load of wash, indulge in a few.

Makes 12 cookies

COOKIES

4 cups all-purpose flour, plus more for rolling

3 tablespoons granulated sugar

Pinch of salt

2 cups (4 sticks) unsalted butter, at room temperature, plus more for the baking sheet

4 large egg yolks

1 cup sour cream

FILLING

2 cups (4 sticks) unsalted butter, at room temperature

1 cup Crisco

2 pounds powdered sugar

¾ cup whole milk, at room temperature

1 teaspoon vanilla extract

1 (7-ounce) jar marshmallow creme

Make the cookies: In a large bowl, mix together the flour, granulated sugar, and salt. Use two butter knives to cut the butter into the flour mixture until fully combined. Add the egg yolks and sour cream, and mix well. Wrap the dough in wax paper and chill overnight in the refrigerator.

The next day, when you're ready to bake the cookies, preheat the oven to 400°F. Grease a baking sheet with butter or line it with parchment paper. Wrap 12 clothespins in aluminum foil.

Cut off one section of the dough and use a rolling pin to roll out the piece on a floured surface to a ⅛-inch thickness. Cut into strips roughly 1 inch wide and 4 inches long, and wrap each strip around a clothespin, covering the entire clothespin except for the round end.

Place the clothespins on the prepared baking sheet about 1 inch apart, and bake for 8 to 10 minutes, or until slightly browned. Allow them to cool on the baking sheet, and then slide the cookies off the clothespins, pulling them over the round end.

Meanwhile, make the filling: In a large bowl with an electric mixer or using a stand mixer, cream together the butter, Crisco, powdered sugar, milk, and vanilla for 10 minutes. Add the marshmallow creme and beat until only just combined. Chill the filling in the refrigerator for at least 30 minutes to make it easier to work with.

Using a pastry bag fitted with a tip, carefully pipe the filling into the cookies. Refrigerate the cookies in an airtight container until served.

GREYHOUND

Why not drink my favorite cocktail in my favorite place, the laundry room? I highly recommend it.

Makes 1 drink

Ice
3 tablespoons vodka (see Note)
Grapefruit juice

Salt, for rimming the glass (optional)

Fill a tumbler with ice and add the vodka. Add grapefruit juice to fill the glass and stir. If you prefer a Salty Dog, add salt to the rim of the glass.

Note: I recommend using better-quality vodka than what you usually use in the laundry room.

Outdoor Spaces

WILMA'S POTATO SALAD

Just typing *Wilma's Potato Salad* makes me want to skip work today and get cooking. This is hands down the best potato salad I've ever had, and I bet it will become your favorite as well. The dressing is next level. In fact, my brother loves this so much that Mom makes it for him for his birthday every year. And while this recipe makes a lot, don't worry: You and your pals or loved ones will eat it all.

Serves 8

DRESSING

½ cup sugar

1 tablespoon cornstarch

1 teaspoon dry mustard

½ teaspoon kosher salt

¾ cup water

¼ cup white vinegar

2 large eggs, slightly beaten

1 cup mayonnaise

SALAD

6 medium white potatoes, peeled, cooked, cooled, and cut into ½-inch cubes

5 hard-boiled eggs, diced

¼ cup shredded onion with juices

¼ cup chopped fresh parsley

1½ teaspoons kosher salt

½ teaspoon freshly ground black pepper

½ teaspoon paprika, for serving

Make the dressing: Add all dressing ingredients except for the mayonnaise to a heavy saucepan and cook over medium heat until thick and bubbly. Transfer the mixture to a medium bowl, cover the surface of the bowl with plastic wrap, and set aside to cool. When completely cool, stir in the mayonnaise.

Make the salad: In a large bowl, mix together all the salad ingredients except the paprika, tossing gently. Add the dressing and stir until well coated. Garnish the salad with paprika and serve.

BEAN SALAD

If your grandma grew up in the South, she likely makes or made this salad. This sweet and vinegary recipe is Granny Dude's version. We ate it on the regular—during weekdays, sure, but also at picnics, barbecues, and church basement dinners. When I was a kid, our local Kentucky Fried Chicken served a version of this as well.

Serves 8

SALAD

1 (15-ounce) can green beans, drained

1 (15-ounce) can wax beans, drained

1 (15-ounce) can garbanzo beans, drained

1 (15-ounce) can red kidney beans, drained

2 celery stalks, sliced

1 large white onion, sliced and separated into rings

1 green bell pepper, diced

1 red bell pepper, diced

DRESSING

1½ cups sugar

½ teaspoon paprika

1 cup white vinegar

½ cup extra-virgin olive oil

½ teaspoon red pepper flakes

Make the salad: In a large bowl, combine all the salad ingredients and set aside.

Make the dressing: In a small bowl or large measuring glass, whisk together all the dressing ingredients until the sugar is dissolved.

Pour the dressing over the salad, toss until the salad is coated with dressing, and serve.

Garage

POPCORN BALLS

I've eaten these popcorn balls, made regularly by a family friend, practically my entire life. And because I grew up watching *A Charlie Brown Thanksgiving*, during which Chuck and his pals eat popcorn, I've always associated these treats with winter holidays. (Although I did bring them to school once for Halloween.) Easy and fun to make, these popcorn balls owe their super-white appearance to a surprising ingredient: baking soda. When I make them today, I often mix in dried cranberries, nuts, sprinkles, or caramel chips right before I pour in the syrup.

Makes 12 balls

1 cup sugar
½ cup light corn syrup
¼ cup (½ stick) butter
½ teaspoon salt
1 teaspoon vanilla extract
½ teaspoon baking soda

12 cups freshly made popcorn (from about 6 tablespoons kernels)
Neutral oil, such as grapeseed or canola, for shaping the balls (optional)

In a heavy medium saucepan, combine the sugar, corn syrup, butter, and salt. Bring to a boil over medium heat, stirring constantly; continue stirring and boiling for 2 minutes. Remove the mixture from the heat and stir in the vanilla and baking soda.

Pour the syrup mixture over the popcorn, coating the corn well. While wearing plastic disposable gloves or plastic bags on your hands, grab a handful of popcorn and shape it into a ball; it can help to add a bit of oil to the gloves, if desired. Repeat with the remaining popcorn; you should have enough to make a dozen balls.

Allow the popcorn balls to cool completely, wrap in wax paper, and tie each with a ribbon.

ACKNOWLEDGMENTS

Patric and Karin wish to thank: Everyone at Harvest, especially Deb Brody and Emma Effinger, who saw the promise of *House Love*, championed our ideas, and cheered on the writing; plus the entire editorial, marketing, publicity, and production teams, whose efforts have made the publishing process so easy and seamless. Thanks to all of you for bringing *House Love* this far. We're also grateful to HarperAudio's Abigail Marks—it's such fun to hear our words aloud!

The entire team at Levine Greenberg Rostan Literary Agency—major kudos are especially deserved by Daniel Greenberg, who believed in our efforts right from the beginning, plus Tim Wojcik, Miek Coccia, and Melissa Rowland. We wouldn't be here without you!

Zach Harris, whose clever and charming illustrations enliven these pages. (We couldn't figure out a way to work in the goat this time around, but know you've goat a fan in each of us.)

Thanks too to Chuck Klosterman, Sarah Murphy, and Rebecca Bell Sorenson, three of our cheerleaders who've provided enthusiastic insights since our early *Laundry Love* days.

Patric wishes to thank: First off, I have to thank Karin. You really get to know someone when you work together on a project like a book—and to want to do it again!? I wouldn't have wanted to do it with anyone else, so thank you so much, Karin.

I also must thank the scores of clients, customers, friends, and others who asked questions about caring for the home that gave me so many jumping-off points for the book.

The most sincere thanks to everyone who loved *Laundry Love* and encouraged this second book by asking to read more.

Ross, thank you for letting me talk to you about this book, and for being my supportive better half.

Daina Amborn, Siah Camara, Tresa Garr, Martha Gingris, and Matthew Rodriquez—thank you for taking such incredible care of the store and our amazing customers.

Thank you, Kelly Ripa, Mark Consuelos, Ryan Seacrest, Michael Gelman, Jan Weiner, David Mullens, Marie Haycox—you sure know how to change a guy's life. I am so, so lucky.

Jane Latman, Loren Ruch, Sarah M. Thompson, Kyle Davis, Chelsey Rieman, Lynne Davis, Kelly Rivezzi, Christina Federowicz, Mariah Bowers, Dale Jolly, Abbi McCallum, Ben and Erin Napier, Mallorie Rasberry, Maureen McCormick, Andy and Maria Awes, everyone at Committee Films, Zak Hanson, Courtney Reistad, and Matt Schaeffer—I couldn't be the Laundry Guy without you!

Jura Koncius, John Kenney, Helen Carefoot, Meg St-Esprit McKivigan, Alison Stewart, Ellen Byron, Diana Dickson, Joel Seidman, Perri Ormont Blumberg, Jason Matheson, Ted Johnsen, Marah Eakin, Kevin Tibbles, Tamron Hall, Anne Bogel, Zibby Owens, and Francis Lam, thank you for shining the spotlight on my love of laundry, *Laundry Love*, and so much more.

Thank you too to Cassandra Sethi, Glory Edim, Kara Nesvig, Megan Mikkelsen, Charmaie Gordon, Sue Campbell, Connie Nelson, Nancy Ngo, Sarah Hagman, Bob Phibbs, Terri Schlichenmeyer, Juliet Russell, Julia Zerull, Jada Jackson, Miriam DiNunzio, Kristina Miller, Hannah Claeson, Hannah Jackson, Adam Uren, Natalie Ryder, David Driscoll, Terrance Griep, Taylor Peterson, Tammy Hernandez, Amy Nelson, Zoe Vanderweide, Dory Chevlin, Kristina Miller, Molly Guthrey, Natalie Michie, Kathy Berdan, Lois Alter Mark, Chris Hrapsky, Gordon Severson, Bridget Harrison, Sam Silverman, Deborah Duncan, Nicoletta Richardson, Lauren Wellbank, Ashley Abramson, Arianna LaBarrie, Karla Walsh, Kristi Piehl, Heath Recela, Rachel Bulman, Danielle Calma, Laura Fenton, Bruce Beggs, Morgan Noll, Jodi Helmer, Sherri McConnell, Lesley Kennedy, Brian Althimer, Cory Heppola, Lauren Levy, Grant Wenkstern, Lori Barghini, and Julia Cobb.

Thank you for helping make my store run, Christine Jones, Ellen Zeigler, Tami Mitchell, Chris Boys, Heather Ludwig, Scott Erikson, Melissa Smith, Briana DeRosa, Amy Weber, Beth Ahlmquist, Tana Erickson, Karen VanMeter, and Beverlee Dacey.

Thank you, thank you, Heather Ryan, Dan Click, Ellen Shafer, Amy Sperling, Mary Riley, Kathy Ekberg, Chi Chi Larue, Happy Peris, Suzanne

Garry, Amy Campbell Lamphere, Taylor Swift, Raleigh Glassberg, Rhonda Rhodes, Vern Melke, Kevin and Katie Dixon and Gus and Wyland, Gladys Mckenzie, Lisa Wesner, Dianne Ferguson, Glenna Maggard, Shelly Kelly, John Whaley, Shelly Chandler, Daune Stinson, Angie Hughes, Mikayla Hughes, Jordyn Hughes, Lisa Taylor, Triple Five and the Mall of America (thanks for the opportunity to have a store somewhere truly magical!), Lauren Lieber, Seth McNaughton, Ken O'Brien, Marsha Johnson, Julie Menk, Meghan Haapala, Amy Bishop, Marsha Sussman, Marlys Coady, Jennifer Hassen Staub, Mark Oyass, Eric Orner, Matt Fox, Josh Gair, Tony Wood, Marketplace Events, Shelly Gepfert, and, forever, Chris Navritil.

To all my Grayson friends, thanks for the support—you believed in me long ago!

And I send so much gratitude to Jarrod and Stephanie Richardson, Tim, Laura, Lee, and Walker Riddle, Heather Sauber, Lenore Wright, Brian Stamper, Kiley and Lantz Powell, Patrick Condon, Andy Flesherl, Todd and Carmel Lenhard, Erin and John Rodriquez, Suzanne Hall, and, lastly, but certainly with the ultimate regard, my parents, Ron and Nancy Richardson, and Harmie and Wilma Justice.

Karin wishes to thank: Patric, the best book partner I could ask for. Your vision, imagination, hilarity, and kindness make writing a book a total delight—this time, last time, and next time!

Thom, who's been making a home with me for thirty-plus years. Love you, love our kids, and love our life together. *Gute Nacht!*

Gabi, Joey, and Mia, who bring such joy to your parents' lives. We're in awe of the people you are, and are becoming. So proud of you every day and twice on Sunday when you share your news. Love you!

Dad and Mom, who taught me how to create a home—welcoming, beautiful, colorful, and sometimes messy. It was, and is, so good. Thanks, Dad, for believing in me from the get-go.

Sarah and Bob, the dearest of friends. A double thanks for all the fun we've shared throughout the years, including celebrating countless New Year's Eves, getting sopping wet at the Macy's parade, kissing fish in the Boundary Waters, and enjoying a holiday at "Samantha's vacation house." (Sorry I left off you wonderful people from my thank-yous last time around.)

Buddy (a posthumous thank-you) and Bo, my devoted office pals.

All my friends and family members. You know who you are. Thank you, thank you.

INDEX